The Development of Constitutional Guarantees of Liberty

The Development of

Constitutional Guarantees of Liberty

BY ROSCOE POUND

Yale University Press, New Haven and London

© 1957 by Yale University Press, Inc.
Fourth printing, June 1963
Printed in the United States of America by
The Carl Purington Rollins Printing-Office of the
Yale University Press, New Haven, Connecticut.
All rights reserved. This book may not be
reproduced, in whole or in part, in any form
(except by reviewers for the public press),
without written permission from the publishers.
Library of Congress catalog card number: 57-6343

Preface

IN HIS BOOK, *The Struggle for Judicial Supremacy* (1941), Mr. Justice Jackson told us that in Great Britain "to observe civil liberties is good politics and to transgress the rights of individuals or the minority is bad politics." He added: "In the United States I cannot say that this is so." Hence he concludes that the Supreme Court must have the support of a vigorous and enlightened public opinion if it is to uphold civil liberties.

But what may perhaps serve us as the English deep-seated jealousy of infringement of individual and minority rights does in Great Britain is a like deep-seated American respect for law, a traditional expectation that things will be done in accordance with the law of the land and so of the Constitution as an ultimate pronouncement as to what that law is. The guarantees of liberty in American constitutions are not and are not thought of as exhortations as to how government should be carried on or its agencies will operate. They are precepts of the law of the land backed by the power of the courts of law to refuse to give effect to legislative or executive acts in derogation thereof. Thus violation of these secured liberties must amount in effect to a revolution in order to overthrow them. Any considerable infringement of guaranteed individual or minority rights appears to involve much more than overriding a pronouncement of political ethics in a political instrument. It involves defiance of fundamental law; overthrow of established law upon which the maintenance of the general security rests.

Today we do not set so much store by the history of institutions as we did in the last century. But the history of development of our constitutional guarantees out of the medieval faith in law, of how the idea of those guarantees became involved in the very idea of law, and of how that idea maintained itself against masterful monarchs and in eras of profound social and economic change to become the law of the land in formative America, is the story I have tried to tell.

It remains to say that these lectures are published substantially as delivered at Wabash College in 1945.

R.P.

24 April, 1956

Contents

Preface   V

1. In Medieval England   1

2. The Era of the Tudors and Stuarts   27

3. In the American Colonies   55

4. From the Revolution to the Constitution   82

Source Materials Illustrating the Text   112

Index   201

I

In Medieval England

AT THE OUTSET it may be asked, what is meant by "liberty"? In the nineteenth century there was no difficulty in answering that question. Kant's idea of the liberty of each —the free self-assertion of each—limited only by the like liberty of all, subject only to the possibility of like free self-assertion by all, was generally accepted. Liberty was a condition in which free exercise of the will was restrained only so far as necessary to secure a harmonious coexistence of the free will of each and the free will of all others. But I am not speaking of the Kantian idea of liberty, in which my generation was brought up. Whatever "liberty" may mean today, the liberty guaranteed by our bills of rights is a reservation to the individual of certain fundamental reasonable expectations involved in life in civilized society and a freedom from arbitrary and unreasonable exercise of the power and authority of those who are designated or chosen in a politically organized society to adjust relations and order conduct, and so are able to apply the force of that society to individuals. Liberty under law implies a systematic and orderly application of that force so that it is uniform, equal, and predictable, and proceeds from reason and upon understood grounds rather than from caprice or impulse or without full and fair hearing of all affected and understanding of the facts on which official action is taken.

Using the term liberty in that sense, I think of four periods in the development of constitutional guarantees of liberty such as we know them. They are: (1.) medieval England—the Conquest to the Reformation; (2.) the era of the Tudors and Stuarts, from the Reformation to the Revolution of 1688; (3.) the American colonies down to the Declaration of Rights of the Continental Congress (1774); and (4.) the era of written constitutions culminating in the federal Bill of Rights (1791). This period might well be taken to extend to the last new state to be admitted with a constitution of its own framing—Oklahoma in 1907. But I stop with the adoption of the first nine amendments to the federal Constitution (1791). From that time to the second decade of the present century we are but developing the applications of the constitutional guarantees as they had grown up from the Middle Ages and from Coke's exposition of them in the seventeenth century. The Fourteenth Amendment did no more than apply a significant provision of the Fifth Amendment to the states, which already had this provision in their own bills of rights, so as to give it the additional protection of the federal courts as against the states. Whether that period has come to an end in the present generation only the future can say. If it has, I see no basis for assured prophecy of what course the development will take in a new period. But thus far, on the whole, all English-speaking peoples have stood firm for what they have regarded as their birthright of liberty.

My approach to the subject in these lectures will be historical—how these guarantees of liberty have in fact grown up and been shaped from century to century by the exigencies of a balance between those who wield the force of organized society and the individuals subject to their

authority. Behind this balance is the maintaining and
furthering of civilization, of the developing of human
powers to constantly greater completeness—the maximum
of human control over external or physical nature and
over internal or human nature of which men are capable
for the time being. It is the latter, the control over human
nature, achieved mastery over internal nature, which has
made our control over physical nature possible; and it has
been achieved and is maintained by·social control, by the
pressure upon each man brought to bear by his fellow men
in groups and associations and relations in order to constrain him to do his part in upholding civilized society
and to deter him from conduct at variance with the postulates of the social order. There is a task of adjusting relations and ordering conduct so that conflicting and over-
lapping claims and demands and desires may be reconciled
or made compatible with each other with a minimum of
friction and waste. This becomes the task of politically
organized society. It comes to be achieved through law.

In adjusting relations and ordering conduct by the systematic application of the force of a politically organized
society we encounter a problem of balance between the
general security and the individual life and between two
basic tendencies in the individual himself which, if one
may use the much abused term "instinct," may be called
the aggressive instinct or tendency to aggressive self-
assertion and the social instinct or tendency to association
and cooperation with one's fellows. In the science of politics it becomes a problem of balance between government
and freedom, the problem to which Kant and those who
followed him in the last century addressed themselves.
Kant looked on freedom as an end and restraint as a means,
so that there should be complete freedom of individual

action except as restraint was needed to permit of general free individual action. We have ceased to think of the matter in this way, but the problem remains. As Lord Acton put it—"Power tends to corrupt, and absolute power corrupts absolutely." To make restraint efficient, men tend to give wide or even absolute powers to officials. In reaction, after experience of abuse of such powers at the expense of the individual life, men tend to limit and circumscribe them. From the time when a king coveted Naboth's vineyard, the real danger to property has not been from thieves but from rapacious rulers. Those set up to maintain social interests have proved to threaten them. But when the guardians of the public weal have been tied down too tight, it has suffered from their ineffectiveness. Thus there have been alternating periods of stress upon the general security and upon the individual life. How the English and ourselves worked upon this problem from the beginning of the twelfth to the end of the eighteenth century is the story I am to tell.

Looking at the peoples with whom law, as we know it today, has arisen and been carried forward, we begin with a kin-organized society. The household ruled by a house father is the original from which develops the larger kin-group ruled over by a patriarchal head and next the kingdom ruled over by a patriarchal king. The idea of the ruler as father of his country is one which long survives. Along with kin-organization, religious organization grows up. The king is high priest of his people; the heads of kin-groups have priestly functions. When, with the rise of political organization, the kings are expelled, a body of priests or a priestly oligarchy may develop which may become a political oligarchy. Thus a politically organized society may be under a patriarchal king, or, as so fre-

quently in a Greek city-state, a tyrant, a more or less absolute ruler with no title to be king. Or it may be under an
oligarchy, a caste derived from the priestly heads of kin-
groups. Or at the other extreme it may be under the
absolute rule of a majority of a popular assembly. After
achieving an inner order, the first need of a politically
organized society is protection against other societies
coveting the same territory or seeking control of trade or
even control over the people of neighboring societies.
Thus there comes to be military organization of society,
sometimes, as in oriental military monarchies, superpos-
ing a military and tax-gathering organization upon local
kin-organized and politically organized societies. In Greece
and in the East after the conquests of Alexander and in
the Hellenistic era these great military autocracies became
the dominant type. They left the administration of justice,
the characteristic function of the state, to the inner order
of local political organizations, and existed only to collect taxes and tribute. St. Augustine said of them that
they were only large-scale robber bands.

In the Greek city-state, the head of the kin-group and
the council of the older, more experienced, and wiser kins-
men had grown into the patriarchal king and his council
of wise men. With the expulsion or disappearance of the
kings, came, in different cities, the rise of tyrants, of
oligarchies, and of absolute rule of majorities in popular
assemblies, so that there was in the classical era a chronic
condition of conflict of demos or oligarchy with tyrant and
of demos with oligarchy. Reflecting on this condition, the
Greek philosophers were impressed by the need of orderly
maintaining of a social *status quo* and of the security of
social institutions, and sought some theory of authority in
an ideal politically organized society. They sought an ideal

which should serve for adjusting relations and ordering conduct by rule and principle and should impose bonds of reason upon those who enacted, upon those who applied, and upon those who were subject to the rules. In the Minos, Socrates tells us that fire burns and water flows in Persia, at Athens, and in Carthage, however much customs and rules of law might differ there. The rising and setting of the sun, the phases of the moon, the succession of day and night and succession of the seasons, with their uniformity, regularity, and predictability, comparable to the regularity and predictability of the conduct of the righteous man, showed an ideal order of things to which the operations of government and administration of justice ought to conform. What has been called the Greek passion for law was a passion for orderly conduct of government according to this ideal. Through the Roman law and the authority of Aristotle, Greek philosophy of social control was a strong influence on the later Middle Ages and in political philosophy until recent times. The Romans developed social control through law, as we understand it today. But the Roman law with which the formative era of the later Middle Ages came in contact was the codified law of the eastern Roman empire—the codification under Justinian. It was the codification of the law of the empire in which all the power of the magistrates, and so of judging, of issuing edicts, and of proposing laws, and in consequence complete lawmaking, law-interpreting, and law-applying authority, were concentrated in an autocratic ruler. In western Europe this polity came in contact with the Germanic polity of local and national assemblies of free men and of the feudal lord and his chief retainers. At the Norman Conquest the Duke of Normandy, become king of England, came in contact with the Anglo-Saxon

polity of the local assemblies of free men and the national
assembly and the king and his chief retainers as his wise
councillors. Moreover, this contact took place under the
influence of the medieval faith in custom.

Throughout the course of development which leads to
the beginnings of the system of Anglo-American law or, as
we call it, the common law, there is the problem of, on the
one hand, effective ordering of conduct in a civilized society, and, on the other hand, such limitations of and
checks upon those to whom that ordering is committed
as to preserve due balance between the general security
and the individual life.

Of the two chief systems of law in the world of today
one, the modern Roman or civil law, is characteristically
administrative; the other, the English or common law,
is characteristically judicial. In antiquity, while originally
the ultimate lawmaking power was theoretically in the
Roman people, the Roman law grew chiefly through the
edicts of the magistrates and the writings of the juris-
consults. The Roman king, and the judicial magistrate
who succeeded him, did not decide cases in person. The
issue to be tried was framed before him. But he then appointed a *judex* to hear and decide the case. The latter
was not a lawyer and got expert advice on the law from
a jurisconsult. There was no strong permanent bench
of judges. When under the empire there began to be regular and permanent judges they were administrative officials. In legal theory the emperor was the first citizen of
Rome to whom the whole power of all the magistrates
had been delegated by a statute. Thus the theory of the
legal order was administrative. The adjusting of relations
and ordering of conduct was in the hands of administrative
officials who gave written directions to the judges how to

decide and determined by edicts the cases in which actions could be brought and the grounds on which defenses would be allowed.

On the other hand, in the Germanic polity the king had a power of administering justice in person. He could be appealed to directly and could decide cases according to the customary law. The English king sat in his court and decided important controversies and when later the king's court developed into a system of courts, the judges in those courts were his delegates, not to execute his will, but to decide cases according to the common custom of England, as the king was bound to do when he sat in person. Whereas in the final Roman theory law proceeded from the emperor—was made by him—in the English theory it was pre-existing and was found by the king or by his justices and applied to the cases before them as something binding on them no less than on the parties.

As a result of this difference of attitude towards the law, the one system thinking of it as wholly the product of the government, the other thinking of a fundamental law binding the agencies of government, there is a characteristic difference as to declarations of rights and guarantees of liberties in the two systems. In the modern Roman system they are hortatory. They are exhortations addressed to the agencies of government as to how they ought to act. In the common-law system they are precepts of the supreme law of the land, binding citizen and official alike and enforceable by the courts in ordinary proceedings at the suit of persons aggrieved. Not long ago the federal government took possession of a private business through the army. The proprietors at once went into court with an ordinary legal proceeding against those who immediately acted and, challenging the legality of the seizure, obtained a decree of the court in their favor. Compare with this the incident of arrest of the deputies (members of the lower house of the legislative body) by Napoleon III, then president of France. One of the deputies stood out in front of the soldiers and read the constitution to them. But the executive was judge of its own powers. No one could do more than protest. The executive prevailed. In the one system the remedy for action in excess of lawful powers is an action for damages, a suit for injunction, or a writ of quo warranto. In the other it is insurrection, rebellion, or revolution.

With these preliminary ideas, we come immediately to the rise of legal guarantees of liberty in medieval England.

Medieval society was relationally organized. But it was in contact with the ideas of a highly developed, politically organized society, the Roman empire, which had embraced all but the whole civilized world of its day and still survived in the eastern Roman empire at Constantinople. Thus in the later Middle Ages two ideas of law came into competition. The Institutes of Justinian, an authoritative legislation for the empire, laid down that what the emperor pleased had the force of law. The Digest of Justinian, likewise authoritative legislation for the empire, laid down that the emperor was *legibus solutus,* absolved from the laws. On the other hand, the Germanic law was thought of as a quest of the justice and truth of the Creator. As Bracton put it, the king ought not to be under any man but to rule under God and the law. The church achieved on the Roman model a highly developed religious organization of Christendom. The theologian-philosophers of the church developed from Greek philosophy and Roman law a doctrine of natural or ideal law, of universal validity, of which human laws were only declaratory. It was laid down in the philosophical treatises that the law of the state could not derogate from the principles of natural law. But, as D'Aguesseau, chancellor of France, said later, in view of the political organization of his time, that was a difficult and dangerous question. There was nowhere for an individual to go if a positive rule laid down by the king contravened principles of natural law. This should be compared with the way in which English jurists and judges from the thirteenth century on steadfastly opposed the law of the land to royal encroachment and oppressive action of the king's agents.

As the church organized all Christendom as a universal religious society, the universities, in which the Roman law of Justinian was taught after the twelfth century and from which the Roman law gradually spread over the Continent, postulated all Christendom as an empire—the empire of the Christian emperors, Constantine and Justinian. It need not be said that although the universities did succeed in establishing the Roman law (as they made it into the modern Roman law) as a universal law, the idea of all Christendom as one politically organized society was not achieved as a political fact. It remained an academic postulate, becoming a juristic ideal. Instead in the sixteenth century separate, centralized, politically organized states arose to become the nations of the next three centuries and the separate, independent state became the paramount organ of social control. In England, the idea of all Christendom as an empire did not even become a legal ideal.

English law was a law of the courts, a law of the lawyers and judges, taught in the societies of lawyers which have come down from the Middle Ages to England of today. The law of the Continent was a law of the universities, a law of professors and academic commentators, taught from the texts of Justinian. Thus the lawyers on the Continent were trained in an academic tradition of interpreting Justinian's codification as legislation binding on all Christendom as an empire. English lawyers were trained in a tradition of a common custom of England, ascertained, declared, and administered in the king's courts. The one thought of law as proceeding from the ruler, whose will was law, although he ought to will what the ideal natural law prescribed. The other thought of the ruled and the officials and agents of the ruler alike as under a fundamental law of the land having a higher authority and ascertained rather than made.

But what became the established English doctrine was not settled without a struggle. There was a severe contest between the feudal idea of organization and the political idea derived from Rome, with the church favoring the political idea so far as it made for universality, but opposing it so far as it attributed absolute powers to temporal rulers, at variance with the dictates of Christian morals, at variance with the jurisdiction of the church, and in conflict with the relations of the church to the individual Christian.

As Duke of Normandy, William the Conqueror had long been at work imposing a measure of discipline upon the barons who held of him and working out an efficient government for his duchy. As king of England he had the experience, the strength of character, and the will to organize a strong central government in his realm. Through the great survey known as Domesday Book he established the crown as the ultimate landlord. Thus he was both political ruler and paramount landlord, and in that time, in a relationally organized society, the latter was the more significant position. But the mere fact that he was in this relational position toward all Englishmen had momentous consequences, as later developed. The relation of lord and man involved reciprocal rights and duties. It had always to be asked what was customary and reasonable and fair in that relation. Here was opportunity for clash between the role of ruler and the role of landlord; between the Roman imperial idea and the Germanic idea, here reinforced by the natural-law idea of the later medieval theological philosophers. I have already spoken of the proposition of Bracton that the king was under God and the law. Bracton was a clergyman (an archdeacon) but was also a lawyer and a judge. In that famous text we can see him speaking both in his clerical and in his judicial capacity. That it was a commonplace at the time is suggested by another book of the same century, the Mirror of Justices, a book of no intrinsic merit or authority, which however passed into the current of our legal thought in the contests between the courts and the crown in the seventeenth century and so helped form our Anglo-American public law. In the chapter of the Mirror on abuses the first and chief abuse noted is "that the king is above the law, whereas he ought to be subject to it, as it is contained in his oath."

After the conquest the national council, which had been the assembly of the wise men of the nation, became instead the king's court of his feudal vassals. The king's revenue became chiefly feudal aids and incidents of tenure. The Middle Ages did not distinguish jurisdiction and ownership, *imperium* and *dominium*. The feudal lord had jurisdiction by virtue of ownership; as landlord he was also ruler and judge. Thus, as the feudal landlord of whom all land in the kingdom was held, the king became the head and source of all jurisdiction. As the books put it, he was the fountain of justice. Also there was a centralization of administration in his court. First financial administration was organized and put in an efficient system. Then the administration of justice was more and more taken from the local courts, which had come down from before the Conquest, and the courts of the local lords. Here were the materials for absolute monarchy such as developed on the Continent. The king's court, whose counsel and consent were the only limitations on his authority or checks on his power, was made up of his vassals. Even the spiritual lords were to do homage to him for their possessions and in token of their secular dependence. But alongside of this feudal position was his customary position, surviving the Conquest. He was not only feudal overlord, he was king of the nation, the son of the kin. His council was the traditional assembly of the wise men of the nation. The laws by which he ruled were the settled customs which his people claimed from him as of right their own at his coronation. Quite apart from the feudal organization the people were bound to him by oath and he to them by the promises at his coronation and by charter of liberties. The king was fountain of justice. He was not fountain of law.

This combination of new and old relations imposed on the king a heavy burden of business and required appointment of a minister to represent him in the kingdom as the sheriff from before the Conquest represented him in the shire. This minister was called justiciar. He was the representative of the king in all affairs. In the king's absence he was regent of the kingdom. Whether the king was present or absent the justiciar was the head of administration of finance and of justice. Under him there was a body of what might be called secretaries: a body of king's clerks or chaplains (for those were times when reading and writing were confined to the clergy), the chief of whom was called chancellor and later became, as it might be put, the king's secretary of state for justice. But William I carried on a very great part of the business of the state in person. He was strong enough to appoint a great baron to be justiciar. Under the less capable William Rufus the justiciar became prime minister, and instead of a great baron a chaplain or clergyman-lawyer favorite of the king held that great office.

So far as any king of England could be, William the Conqueror was an absolute irresponsible ruler. He was a strong, determined, hard-working man, wise enough not to be a tyrant although he had his hand in every part of the business of the kingdom. On the other hand, his successor, William Rufus, was the worst type of tyrant. He lacked his father's capacity for business, and the government of his justiciar was irresponsible and wantonly oppressive. His brother and successor, Henry I, was as able as their father, the Conqueror, and as despotic as William Rufus. But he organized administration and thus put a check upon his own caprice.

"Form," says Jhering, "is the sworn enemy of caprice, the twin sister of liberty. . . . Fixed forms are the school of discipline and order, and thereby of liberty itself." Form and routine are the only safeguard of a people under an autocracy. Imposition of form and routine upon those who exercised the king's authority was a step toward the supremacy of law which was to become characteristic of the English polity.

Under the three Norman kings, the king and the people supported one another in establishing and maintaining a national system as against the disintegrating system of local feudal jurisdictions. The great vassals of the crown were their common enemy. Hence William Rufus and Henry I, when hard pressed by their vassals, were able to buy the help of the country by promises. The king feared to increase the jurisdiction of the great barons and so upheld the people in their customary liberties. In the second section of the Charter of Liberties granted by Henry I the tenants of the barons are to be secured against their landlords, and in the fourth section the barons are to "hold themselves in check towards their tenants." A century later the barons are claiming liberties from the king and now the interest of the people at large is with the barons. In the Articles of the Barons, leading to Magna Carta, the liberties of the free man, not simply of the king's tenant in chief, are regularly guaranteed.

Under Henry I we get the organization of the king's court which is to become the king's courts of common law in which the liberties of the Englishman come to be enforced, and the first charter of liberties in which those liberties are to be defined. Henry I organized the administration of the justiciar. He now had a staff selected from the barons or vassals of the crown more nearly connected with the royal household or qualified to act as judges by their knowledge of the law. They made up the highest court of the nation; the king's court, attendant upon the king in practice, and in its derivative, the court of King's Bench, long afterwards in theory held before the king in person. In time this king's court separates into the High Court of Parliament, legislature and in its upper branch supreme court of judicature, and what becomes the courts of justice. But already it is on one side a sort of judicial committee of the whole court of vassals, by which all appeals are decided and to which all suits may be called upon application of the suitors. Its functions are still undifferentiated. It has to do with assessment and collection of revenue. In its capacity of royal council it takes part in the revision and registration of the laws and charters which it attests. Below it there is still the old judicial machinery from before the Conquest, the county courts, the hundred courts, and the local franchises by virtue of which local landlords held courts and administered justice to their tenants. Taxation and the making of laws are out of its sphere. They belong to the king and the national assembly, now composed of his vassals. But the court out of which sprang the common-law courts was manned by judges of rank and dignity so that from the beginning the common-law judges were strong enough to uphold the traditional liberties against the most masterful kings.

Under the Norman kings the functions of the national council were more nominal than real. But the form of participation in authorizing taxation and in legislation was retained. In the amendment of old laws by William I and Henry I the immemorial counsel and consent of the barons is recited, as to this day a statute recites that it is enacted by the advice and consent of the lords, spiritual and temporal, and the commons. Thus from the beginning of the English polity there is a protest against the doctrine of the Romanist lawyers of the Continent, based on devolution of all legislative power upon the king, that what pleases the king has the force of a law. But the further development in this direction belongs to political history.

On the other side, the Charter of Liberties of Henry I defines liberties in characteristic English fashion not by abstract pronouncements but by dealing with concrete abuses, from which lawyers may derive principles to meet later and newer abuses. The Charter of Henry I has to do immediately with the autocratic government under his father and particularly his brother and the extortionate exactions and abusive exercise of powers in connection with the incidents of tenure. Reliefs payable by the heir who succeeded to an estate, fines payable upon alienation of an estate, aids payable when the lord had to be ransomed or sustained an extraordinary expense on making his eldest son a knight or when his eldest daughter was married, guardianship of infant heirs, and sale of the marriage of heirs and heiresses were sources of royal revenue and afforded means of unreasonable exactions, beyond what was customary, of wasting estates, and of oppression of widows and daughters of deceased tenants. These incidents of tenure were to be enforced in accordance with the provisions of the charters providing for them and according to the customary law.

We may date the rule of law definitely from the reign of Henry II. He was by nature a lawyer and a man of business. From the beginning of his reign he set out to put order on a permanent basis. By a steady system of reforms he made the administrative machinery, which under Henry I had been regulated by routine, part of a constitution of government set forth in laws. He sought to carry to completion an organization of government which should make return to the anarchy of independent feudal lords and jurisdictions impossible. The obstacles to this policy were opposition of the barons and of the clergy. He had to compel the barons to suffer restriction of their hereditary jurisdictions to the narrowest limits. He had to make the clergy, in all matters not purely spiritual, subject to the ordinary process of the law. He succeeded in the contest with the barons. In the contest with the clergy he was humiliated. Yet he succeeded in his ultimate aim of reducing all men to equality before the same system of law. Perhaps the most significant of his achievements was the grand jury which provided efficient detection and prosecution of offenders while protecting individuals against unfounded prosecutions either private or by officials of government, and the trial jury which superseded trial by battle and the crude ordeals and compurgation and made possible rational instead of mechanical trial.

John was an able soldier but a bad ruler. His recurrence to extortionate exactions and oppressive practices in the enforcement of incidents of tenure and his high-handed, unlawful seizures of property for his use brought on a contest with the barons in which they found a program for the redress of grievances in the Charter of Henry I. They compelled John to renew this charter with large additions, and in securing what they claimed as their constitutional rights they bound the king to observe the same rules towards all free men.

The ground plan to which the common-law polity has built ever since was given by the Great Charter. It was not merely the first attempt to put in legal terms what became the leading ideas of constitutional government. It put them in the form of limitations on the exercise of authority, not of concessions to free human action from authority. It put them as legal propositions, so that they could and did come to be a part of the ordinary law of the land invoked like any other legal precepts in the ordinary course of orderly litigation. Moreover, it did not put them abstractly. In characteristic English fashion it put them concretely in the form of a body of specific provisions for present ills, not a body of general declarations in universal terms. Herein, perhaps, is the secret of its enduring vitality. Like the Constitution of the United States it is a great legal document. Like the Constitution it lent itself to development by lawyers' technique. It did not foreclose legal development by universal abstract clauses. It did not seek to anticipate and provide for everything in time to come. When recent historians, affecting to overthrow the lawyer's conception, tell us that its framers meant no more than to remedy this or that exact grievance of a time and place and class by a particular legal provision framed to the exigencies of that grievance, they tell us no more than that the method of the Great Charter is the method of English law in all ages. The frame of mind in which it was drawn was nothing less than the frame of mind of the common-law lawyer; the frame of mind that looks at things in the concrete, the frame of mind that prefers to go forward cautiously, on the basis of experience, from this case to the next case as justice in each case seems to require. Exactly because it is an example of the sure-footed Anglo-Saxon's habit of dealing with things as they arise and in the light of experience, it has been able to maintain itself as the foundation of English and American public law for seven centuries.

Historians now tell us that Magna Carta goes back by way of the Charter of Liberties of Henry II and the like charters of Stephen and Henry I to the Charter of Liberties of Cnut. But this is only its formal pedigree. In substance it is another thing. In substance it formulates ideas and realizes principles which are at the foundation of medieval social and political life. Thus if its formal roots are in the Anglo-Norman writ-charter and the Anglo-Saxon writ, its material roots are in the whole legal and political thought of the twelfth century and so in the Germanic law as affected by the law of the church and by the Roman law. Exacted by a combination of landowners, church, and merchants, and granted by a king, it recognizes the centralized judicial and administrative system which made the common law possible, but is not exactly a constitution, nor a statute, nor a treaty, nor a compact, nor a declaration of rights, and yet has something of all of these. What stands out is the legal quality. For in the Middle Ages men thought of human welfare in the aspect of legality as distinctly as today they think of it in the aspect of utility. Men thought of society as held together by a system of reciprocal rights and duties, involved in relations, and half human, half divine. Authority was partitioned between church and state. The state was divinely ordained as a remedy for sin and an agency for promoting justice and right. The supremacy of law, a fundamental dogma of our common law, one, moreover, which we trace back to Magna Carta, is but the supremacy of right divorced at the Reformation from its theological element.

John used the powers of the crown and the administrative machinery which the genius of his father had provided not for wise national purposes but to oppress every class in society. He exacted more from the barons than had been customary. He oppressed the smaller landlords both indirectly through their lords and directly through his administrative officials. He attacked the church, whereas in the medieval polity it was fundamental that church and state were coworkers in maintaining the social order. He made heavy money demands upon the merchants without giving them in return protection and good government. He used the administrative agencies of protection as instruments of extortion. Thus he united all interests and classes against him. Although the Great Charter was exacted by the barons, all these classes were behind it and it sought in characteristic English fashion to give concrete remedies to each for the concrete grievances of each. No less in characteristic English fashion, instead of overthrowing the administrative machinery of Henry II, which John had abused, instead of wrecking orderly government and administration, which had been made instruments of extortion, the barons demanded and obtained more precise and exact definition of the reciprocal duties and claims in the relation of king and subject, of overlord and tenant in chief, and a body of authoritatively declared legal limitations upon royal employment of the administrative machinery of the realm.

In one aspect the Great Charter is a redress of the grievances of the great landowners, imposing limits of order and reason upon the king's exactions as feudal overlord. But the grievances of the church are put first. It is thus also a redress of the grievances of the church, imposing respect for the then fundamental division of powers between the spiritual and the temporal. In still another aspect it is a redress of the grievances of the merchants and traders, providing for uniform weights and measures, freedom of travel, and freedom from unjust taxation. Most of all, however, and in its general aspect, it is a redress of common grievances of all. It calls for reasonable fines, proportioned to the offense and to the offender. It calls for justice as something of right, not to be sold, denied, or delayed. It calls for security of property, which is not to be taken for the king's purposes without the old customary payment. It calls for security of the person. The free man is not to be imprisoned or banished or outlawed or disseised or deprived of his established privileges without a lawful judgment or otherwise than according to law. These last provisions, coming into our law by way of Coke's commentary on Magna Carta and our American bills of rights, have proved of enduring vitality. Interpreted and applied by American courts in one hundred and fifty years of constitutional legal development, they have proved equal to the constraining of sovereign peoples, organized in sovereign states, to rule under God and the law.

Through these general provisions which, if devised for particular grievances of particular classes in a particular time and place, yet were applicable to like grievances in any time and place, the Great Charter established a system of constitutional government, and so is rightly revered as the source of the surest agency of social and political stability in the modern world and the symbol of that supremacy of law over the agencies of government and those guarantees to the individual man that administrative machinery, while guiding him and protecting him, will not grind him down, which are the proudest possession of Englishmen and their descendants everywhere.

Rights secured by the Great Charter became in their turn the basis or program of new claims which were the subject of struggles running through the whole reign of Henry III. In those struggles they were made good. The next reign sees them accepted by the good faith and defined by the lawmaking and administrative genius of Edward I. The medieval struggle for a constitution ends with his reign. For a generation that great ruler reigned as Henry II had done, showing due respect for constitutional forms but exercising the reality of despotic power. He elaborated and completed the organization of Parliament, of the convocation, of the courts of law, of provincial jurisdiction, as they were to stand substantially for seven centuries. His legislation was so full and well done that the laws of the next three centuries are not much more than an expansion of it. He long retained the substance of royal power, control of finance: the right to impose a compulsory aid or tax upon the towns and the demesnes of the crown without the consent of Parliament. But he was compelled to give these up. The Confirmation of the Charters by Edward I marks the end of a formative period in the political history and begins one of legal political history of the English constitution. Here begins the legal order as a judicially maintained order guaranteeing liberty as it has stood in the English-speaking world since that time.

In the next two centuries the English lawyers and judges steadfastly apply the principles established in the thirteenth century. In a case in 1338 the Court of King's Bench allowed cattle taken in distress for not paying the king's taxes to be replevied from the king's collector because the latter had no warrant. An official could not seize the property of a subject except in the legal manner and under authority of a lawful warrant. If it is said that after all this was no more than insistence by the judges upon a matter of form, the answer is that the form in such cases is a guarantee of the substance. If the official pursues it he is acting within a lawful authority. If he does not, having no lawful authority he is a private trespasser. Compelling him to have and show authority holds him to legal limits on what he does.

In another case about the same time certain persons were convicted in the King's Bench of forcible disseisin, that is, wrongfully putting another out of his freehold with force and arms. Thereupon the court issued a writ of *exegi facias* to outlaw them. The sheriff returned this writ setting forth that the king, by a letter under the privy seal, i.e. a private letter, had instructed him that he

had pardoned the offenders their trespasses and commanded that they should not be molested on that account,
wherefore by reason of the king's message the sheriff had
not executed the writ. The court held that this letter did
not authorize the sheriff to refuse to act under the writ,
and fined him and issued a new one. The king could pardon offenders under the Great Seal. Also he could, when
properly applied to, dispense with some particular provisions of the law in favor of some particular person to
prevent great hardship—a power which was afterwards
exercised by the chancellor and became the basis of the
jurisdiction of the Court of Chancery. If the king had
acted in exercise of this power and so notified the court,
the court would have recalled the writ. But the king in
his individual rather than his official capacity could not
write private letters to the sheriff to interfere with the
due course of justice in the courts.

To appreciate the significance of this case it should be
compared with the practice of *lettres de cachet* in France.
These were letters issued under the privy seal and signed
by the king, countersigned by a minister, authorizing the
imprisonment of someone or giving someone protection
against the course of the law or delaying or stopping legal
proceedings. They could be obtained by any one of sufficient influence with the king or his ministers. Under them
persons might be imprisoned for life or for long periods
on the most frivolous pretexts, for the gratification of private pique or revenge, without any reason being assigned.
We are told that the secretary of state issued them in a
wholly arbitrary fashion and that in most cases the king
was quite unaware of their issue. Indeed, they were often
issued in blank, that is, without containing the name of
the person against whom they were to be used, leaving it

to the person to whom they were given to fill in such name as he liked. How this system operated is well brought out in the story of the count of Monte Cristo. It might easily happen that the person so imprisoned did not know why or at whose instance he was held and that the occasion and reason might be forgotten while he languished in indefinite confinement. The English courts would not tolerate such things.

Sir John Fortescue, who was chief justice under Henry VI and lived a long time in exile in France during the Wars of the Roses as tutor to the Prince of Wales, son of Henry VI, wrote a book somewhere between 1467 and 1471 in which he compares English law with the law in France as to the liberty of the subject. While his picture of the happiness in England and the misery of the peasantry in France may be somewhat overenthusiastic, we have here a picture by a contemporary observer which brings out the achievement of English judicial development and application of the Great Charter.

Thus far I have spoken only of arbitrary action of the crown. But cases of transgression of fundamental law by Parliament have even more significance for American constitutional development. In the medieval polity there was a basic distinction between spiritual and temporal jurisdiction, and this had been guaranteed both by the last chapter of the Great Charter and in the Confirmation of Charters by Edward I. When, therefore, Parliament undertook to provide for the custody of the seal of a religious house otherwise than the provisions of the law of the church, the Court of Common Pleas in 1450 said simply and plainly that the statute was impertinent to be observed and void. Parliament had attempted to do something that the fundamental law put beyond its reach.

Again, in 1506, the Court of Common Pleas refused to give effect to a statute of Henry V which would have had the effect of making the king a parson. No one could be made a parson by a temporal act. The king could not be given any spiritual jurisdiction without the assent of the pope.

In the sixteenth century came the Reformation, the rise of strong centralized national governments in western Europe, and an era of absolute monarchies which marks the seventeenth and eighteenth centuries. In England, Parliament and the courts are in a struggle with the crown until it is settled by the Revolution of 1688 that the English king is still under God and the law. The judicial securing of the rights guaranteed to Englishmen by the Great Charter was seriously threatened. But it had been too thoroughly established in the Middle Ages to be overthrown.

2

The Era of the Tudors and Stuarts

THIS SECOND PERIOD begins in the time of what Maitland
calls the three R's, Renaissance, Reformation, and Reception of Roman law. The humanists of the Renaissance
were not likely to appreciate the enduring qualities of
the English common law. What they could see on the
surface was that its books were written in bad Latin and
worse French, were registers of writs, alphabetical abridge-
ments, and unsystematic reports of discussions of counsel
and judges in framing issues for trial, of decisions of the
superior courts, and of news of the profession along with
privately published collections of statutes, neither complete nor authoritative. There had been no adequate
systematic treatise since Bracton in the thirteenth century. The civil law had been studied in the universities
since the twelfth century. Study of English law was carried
on in the societies of lawyers in severely practical fashion.
The Reformation had struck down half of the fundamental law which the medieval lawyer had regarded as
beyond the reach of temporal lawmaking. It would no
longer be possible for common-law judges to refuse to give
effect to statutes enacted by Parliament on the ground
that they encroached on the domain of the church and
so were "impertinent to be observed." In 1535, the Year
Books, which, whatever they were, at any rate served the
purpose of a continuous report of judicial decision since

the time of Edward I, came to an end. It looked as if
the Reception of Roman law, which was reaching Scot-
land, might reach England also. At any rate, there were
those who were urging it in the reign of Henry VIII.
There were projects for reforming the education of lawyers, projects for a code, and projects for and setting up
of new tribunals not administering the law of the land
nor proceeding according to its ideals. The students of
law were petitioning claiming that the common law was
being set aside for the civil law and that business was
leaving the common-law courts. There seems to have been
for a time a real menace to the continuity of English legal
history. What this might have meant to our regime of
constitutionally guaranteed and judicially maintained
liberty may be seen when we note how hard it was for
the courts to prevail in the contest with the Stuarts in the
next century.

It was a time when old creeds were being discarded,
when old institutions were being overthrown, when men
were in revolt against the past on the shoulders of which
they were standing, and were replacing authority by
reason. That the common law developed from the thirteenth to the fifteenth century could survive in such a
time is a testimony to the vitality of its fundamental ideas.

What was more serious for the common-law tradition of
liberty under law judicially maintained, the time was one
of administrative tribunals with a summary, Romanized
procedure and scant respect for the rights of the individual
Englishman, when those who exercised the powers of
politically organized society were active to achieve results
for the government. The King's Council, the Star Chamber, and the Court of Requests are characteristic tribunals
of this period. They had the appearance of being modern

and in the spirit of the age as compared with the old courts, tied down by formal procedure and bound by an unsystematic body of writs grown up to the exigencies of particular cases and given stability and rigidity by three centuries of application in court and teaching by practicing lawyers.

Relationally organized society was breaking down. The church had been subjected to the king, which would have been regarded a century before as in derogation of the first chapter of Magna Carta. The Wars of the Roses had decimated and two masterful kings had humbled the baronage. Parliament had given the king a power of legislation by proclamation which might have undone the constitutional development which had gone on from the time of Henry III. Monarchs zealous to do things, impatient of medieval legal limitations and, as Shakespeare put it, "rotten parchment bonds," could not but be attracted by the eastern Roman code and the doctrine that the sovereign was not bound by laws. Elsewhere it was a time of rising, absolute, personal government, the France of Francis I, the Spain of Charles V, and an English king could not patiently endure being less a king than the rulers of the two states which were the models for those days.

On the other hand, the individual Englishman was acquiring a new importance and a new sense of independence. The discovery of the New World, exploitation of natural wealth, and expansion of trade and commerce led to adventurous individualism and a competitive acquisitive self-assertion which was impossible in the social organization of the Middle Ages. Authority, as the Middle Ages had relied upon it, had lost its hold. The writings of the fathers of the church, Aristotle, and Justinian were no longer unchallengeable—to be interpreted but not questioned. Private interpretation of the Bible, every man to read it and expound it to himself, involved a claim of primacy for the individual reason. If there were forces at work making for absolutism there were others latent which would make for maintaining and extending the guarantees of individual freedom.

Government under the Tudors was on the whole more arbitrary than under the Plantagenets. Not all of the Plantagenets were strong rulers, while Henry VII, Henry VIII, Mary, and Elizabeth were possessed in high degree of courage and force of will. For over a hundred years they ruled vigorously, often violently, and not infrequently cruelly. As Fortescue had pointed out in his praise of the laws of England, the kings before the Tudors had from time to time sought to rule with a high hand and ignore the legal limits of their authority. Plantagenet and Tudor, as occasion allowed, infringed the rights of individuals, exacted loans and gifts as a mode of taxation, and dispensed with statutes. They even, when Parliament was not sitting, met temporary situations by edicts. Characteristically the English constitution did not precisely define the prerogative. All admitted that there was a body of prerogative. All admitted there were some things beyond the power of the crown. Where lines were to be drawn had to be fought out in the seventeenth century. But there was one circumstance which made it impossible for the Tudors to go far in oppression of the people. They had no armed force at their beck, and as arms were in those days an armed people involved little beyond what was everyday household equipment and so the king was surrounded by an army of his subjects. The array of any county or of a ward of London could overpower what guard the king had or could command. Hence if the laws were not strong enough to restrain him none the less public opinion backed up the laws effectively. From time to time these rulers could treat some individual arbitrarily and even barbarously. But they could not indulge in any general long-continued oppression of the whole people. However tyrannical in their household or their court, they were compelled to be cautious in arousing the temper of the country. Henry VIII could procure the execution of wives or courtiers. But when he sought to impose a heavy financial contribution without the consent of Parliament, he roused an irresistible opposition. He was told that his subjects were English, not French; free men, not slaves. The king's commissioners were mobbed. Armed insurrection was threatened, and the king's officials could raise no force to put it down. Henry VIII remembered Edward II and Richard II and did not persist. Provisions in American constitutions as to the right of the people to bear arms preserve the memory of these episodes.

While the Tudors were hot-tempered and high-spirited, they were not unreasonably obstinate like the Stuarts. Like Edward I they knew when it was time to give in to the insistent demand of the nation for adherence to law. From time to time their rule was resisted but it was not subverted. Yet this very caution, this wise stopping short when it was time to yield, this timely making of concessions which enabled them much of the time to rule despotically, might have gradually enabled encroachments destructive of the constitution. The Stuarts had no such cautious discretion. They obstinately opposed all legal restriction and so brought about their ruin and the establishment of legal guarantees of freedom.

Under the Tudor rulers there were no such conflicts

of the courts with the crown as arose later under the Stuarts. The courts went on deciding as they had done since the fourteenth century. Elizabeth wrote letters to the judges, telling them what it was her will that they do, and inquiring why they had not done it. But when the judges asserted the law and refused to comply, she pushed the matter no further. The significant cases in which the authority of the crown was exceeded were the extortions practiced by Empson and Dudley under Henry VII, royal restrictions on imports under Mary, and certain grants to favorites by Elizabeth.

A statute of Henry VII, which Coke tells us was in contravention of Magna Carta and of "ancient and fundamental law," provided that justices of assize and justices of the peace, without any presentment or findings of a jury, upon a bare information before them on behalf of the king, should have full power and authority in their discretion to hear and determine all offenses and contempts by any person against any statute. Empson and Dudley were justices of the peace and were also made "masters of forfeitures," a new office created for them. Under the statute they extorted enormous sums for the crown by enforcement of antiquated statutes. As masters of forfeitures, in cases where it was claimed that property had accrued to the king, they contrived by making records of untrue claims, altering records, and making false records, to prevent traversing (denying) the claims, so that the owners could only make a petition and a compromise. These cases did not get before the common-law courts. But a short time before his death the king repented and ordered that traverses be allowed in all cases and that such matters should be determined according to the true course of the law. An act of Parliament of the first year of Henry VIII put an end to the taking of evidence in secret in such cases, recited the unlawful practices of Empson and Dudley, and provided for redress of those who had suffered. The statute of Henry VII conferring wide discretionary powers upon justices of assize and justices of the peace was repealed.

Coke tells us that Edward III attempted in many different ways to raise money from merchants or impose charges upon imports without act of Parliament. Parliament succeeded in opposing these attempts, and later statutes provided for lawful customs dues. After that, he tells us, "no king imposed by pretext of any prerogative any charges upon merchandises imported into or exported out of the realm until Queen Mary's time." Philip and Mary granted by letters patent to the corporation of Southampton that no malmsey wine should be imported into the kingdom except at the port of Southampton and provided for a threefold penalty to the crown in cases of violation. Certain foreign merchants brought malmsey wines into the kingdom and landed them elsewhere. Upon this the attorney general brought an information against them in the Exchequer for the penalty. The case was argued before all the judges in the Exchequer Chamber upon demurrer to the information. The judges held that the grant was a restraint of liberty contrary to law and utterly void. Chapter 41 of Magna Carta is cited for the decision. Also, in an information by the attorney general in the Exchequer to recover a sum of 40 shillings a tun, imposed by Queen Mary on French wine brought into England, the court held on demurrer that this was contrary to Magna Carta, which provided that all merchants should be free to come to England and buy and sell "by the ancient and right customs, quit from all evil tolls," except alien enemies in time of war.

Two notable cases were decided in the reign of Elizabeth. In those days there was property in certain offices, paid by fees. Blackstone names offices among "incorporeal hereditaments"; that is, certain offices were hereditary. The holder of the office had an estate in it to him and his heirs. Other offices were held in life estate or for a term. But the estate in the office was property. Certain officials in the Common Pleas held for life offices whereby they were entitled to make certain writs and receive the fees therefor. The duties of officers of this sort were often performed by deputies who did the work and paid the office-holder well for the place. Such being the case, the queen granted to one Cavendish by letters patent a term for years in the office of making all of certain writs, and sent notice to the judges to admit him thereto. This the judges refused to do. Thereupon Cavendish induced her to write a letter to the judges under her signature and private seal commanding them to sequestrate the profits of the office since the grant as well as those to ensue, committing them to someone under bond to Cavendish in the event it should be determined that he was entitled to the office. The judges considered this letter and decided that they could not lawfully act on it because to do so would disseise of their freehold the officers to whom the making of such writs belonged. Certain great men, friends of Cavendish, told the queen of this, and she wrote then another private letter to the judges commanding them to admit him to the office without further delay and leave it to the officers so disseised to recover their offices by action at law. This letter was brought to the judges by two of the queen's favorite courtiers, the lord chancellor, Sir Christopher Hatton, known as the "dancing chancellor" because he was said to have secured his preferment by dancing with the queen, and the Earl of Leicester, then the reigning favorite. They told the judges that the queen had a great desire to provide advancement for Cavendish and had commanded them to hear the judges' answer to the letter. To this the judges answered that they could not obey the letter consistently with their oath to administer justice according to the law of the land.

Upon report of this answer to the queen, she ordered the chancellor (Hatton), the Chief Justice of the Queen's Bench (Sir Christopher Wray), and the Master of the Rolls to hear the judges as to their reasons for disobeying her commands. The judges protested that this calling on them to pass on the question at a private interview, instead of Cavendish's bringing an appropriate legal proceeding to establish his right, if he had one, and having the case decided after argument at which the present office-holders could be heard was out of the course of justice and in consequence they would not answer. It was for the office-holders who were to be disseised to argue. They were then charged with not having obeyed the queen's orders, and replied that the orders were against the law of the land so that no one was bound to obey them, and cited many precedents, including chapter 39 of Magna Carta. The queen, when this was reported to her, had the good sense to drop the matter. It was not heard of further.

But this did not stop the queen's endeavors to provide for courtiers at the expense of her subjects. She tried another experiment in royal grants which came before the courts finally in the reign of her successor.

Under pretense of regulating the playing of cards by men of "mean trades and occupations" (who, I suppose, it was considered ought to be at work and could not afford "idle games"), Elizabeth made a grant to Darcy authorizing him and his agents and deputies to provide playing cards and prohibiting all others for a term of years from importing such cards or making or selling them in the realm. On the strength of this grant Darcy brought an action in the Queen's Bench, setting up the grant and alleging that he had provided cards accordingly, but that notwithstanding the grant the defendant brought cards into the realm and sold them in infringement of the plaintiff's monopoly. To this the defendant pleaded the custom of London (guaranteed by chapter 13 of Magna Carta) that a freeman (i.e. a citizen, one of the corporation of London) might buy and sell all things merchantable, alleged that he was a freeman and merchant of London, that playing cards were things merchantable, and that he bought and sold them accordingly. This was demurred to and the demurrer was twice argued in the last year of the queen's reign and decided in the first year of James I. As counsel put it in argument, the case against the patent had to be argued with caution because one who looked at the majesty of the prince, like one who looked at the sun, would be oppressed by its splendor. Or, as he put it in another way, where one hews above his head chips will fall in his eyes. But the queen had been content to have her grants and patents scrutinized by the courts, as Cavendish's case showed. So Dodderidge, an able lawyer, afterwards Justice of the King's Bench, who, however, was inclined later to be subservient to James I, argued for the defendant. The court held for the defendant, all the judges agreeing that a monopoly was against the common law and contrary to certain acts of Parliament. The grant was held not only contrary to the guaranteed liberties of citizens of London, but an unlawful restraint of liberty. Not the least interesting feature of the case is Coke's comment on the pretentious preamble to the grant. As he says, privileges which in reality are prejudicial to the public welfare often have more specious frontispieces and more pretense of good than good and legal concessions. In time of rising political absolutism these hypocritical preambles are to be seen. Before absolutist ideas obtain some currency such preambles avail nothing. After absolutism is established they are not needed. While absolutism is growing but feels the need of support, they are freely employed. At present, in contrast with earlier practice in America, preambles of this kind have become common.

Such was the condition of the law when James I and his successors undertook to set up in England an absolute monarchy after the fashion of the Continent. In this they were opposed by Parliament on political grounds and by lawyers on legal grounds. Many politicians supported the crown in the long contest; and so did many members of the legal profession, although as Sir Thomas Jones told his royal master, few lawyers were willing to do the king's will on the bench in order to gain a position to which their professional standing and ability did not entitle them. But even these, as a rule, could only be pushed so far. When the king demanded decisions which they could not make consistently with a pretense of law they, too, balked and had to be removed.

We have seen Queen Elizabeth writing letters to the judges and sending emissaries to them in advance of litigation. James I in 1615 began a practice of sounding out the judges and getting their opinions privately in advance of litigation in which the crown was interested. Desiring to have the private opinion of the judges whether Peacham, a Puritan clergyman, who had written a sort of philippic against the government, could be convicted of treason, the king sent Bacon (the attorney general) to procure it. But when the question was put to Coke, then Chief Justice of the King's Bench, he answered that "this auricular taking of opinions, single and apart, was new and dangerous." When, however, the other judges had given their opinions, Coke agreed to give his in writing, and wrote one against the prosecution. He afterwards yielded to the practice of giving opinions to the government in advance, which the king's persistence had established. When, however, the king summoned the judges before the council for refusing to stop proceedings in an ordinary case between party and party when ordered to by royal mandate, Coke, in answer to the question whether he would stay proceedings on a future command of the sort, answered that "when the case should be he would do that which should be fit for a judge to do." He was removed from his position by the king.

Under the succeeding Stuart kings removal of judges for decisions unfavorable to the crown or even for not agreeing in advance to decide as the king desired became a habitual practice. Charles I removed three. Charles II removed ten. James II, in a reign of three years, removed thirteen—more each year than his father had removed in twenty-four years.

Although there were many strong judges on the bench in this period, under Charles II and James II a politics-ridden bench, a seat on which was dependent on doing

what the exigencies of royal government demanded, sank
to the lowest point in English judicial history.

A few examples will tell the story sufficiently. When
Charles I was trying to fill his exhausted treasury by forced
loans he applied to the judges and expected them not only
to pay what they would have had to pay on a legally
granted subsidy but also to sign a paper recognizing the
legality of the collection. Sir Randolph Crewe, Chief
Justice of the King's Bench, refused to sign and was removed. Also Sir John Walter, Chief Baron of the Exchequer, proved too independent and the king forbade
his sitting in court.

Naturally the bad example set by James I and Charles
I was followed by the Long Parliament which impeached
the judges who had decided in favor of the crown in the
ship-money case, although some of them, at any rate, gave
their honest opinions, not without some legal basis, for the
limits of the prerogative were then by no means settled.

To name a few of the judges removed by Charles II, in
1678 he removed four: Sir Vere Bertie, Justice of the Common Pleas, Sir William Wilde, Justice of the King's Bench,
Sir Edward Thurland, Baron of the Exchequer, and Sir
Francis Bramston, Baron of the Exchequer, all of whom
were in the commission for the trial of Reading, indicted
on the testimony of the notorious false witness Bedloe.
Apparently their conduct at the trial was not satisfactory
to the king. The same year he removed Sir Richard Rainsford, Chief Justice of the King's Bench, in order to make
way for Sir William Scroggs, one of the worst names in
English judicial history. Scroggs only escaped impeachment by the dissolution of Parliament and it seemed pru-
dent to the king to remove him, so thoroughly obnoxious

had he become. Sir Francis Pemberton, an excellent lawyer, Chief Justice of the King's Bench, was demoted to the Common Pleas in 1683 as not sufficiently favorable to the crown in the proceeding to forfeit the charter of London. The same year he was removed from the bench entirely for showing "so little eagerness" to convict Lord Russell. He was afterwards one of the counsel for the Seven Bishops. In 1680 Sir Robert Atkyns, Justice of the Common Pleas, was removed for, among other things, denying the king's power to forbid the publication of books without an act of Parliament. William III restored him to the bench as Chief Baron of the Court of Exchequer.

It would take too long to go over the list of judges removed by James II. It includes the chiefs of each of the common-law courts: Sir Edward Herbert, Chief Justice of the King's Bench, removed in 1687 for refusing to sanction royal introduction of military tribunals with authority to inflict capital punishment without an act of Parliament; Sir Thomas Jones, Chief Justice of the Common Pleas, dismissed in 1687 for refusing the king, at his personal solicitation, an advance opinion in favor of a general royal dispensing power; and Sir William Montagu, Chief Baron of the Exchequer, removed along with three of his colleagues in 1686 for opposing the king's opinion that he could do away with the Test Acts by his own will. That the judges and the profession as a whole stood so steadfastly for the law of the land during these four reigns is one of the glories of the common-law bar. Indeed, Cromwell found the lawyers no less determined and after a brief struggle to bend them to his purposes said, "the sons of Zeruiah are too hard for us," and gave them up.

For the seventeenth-century legal and political philosophers the chief question was, how can one man or body of men get authority over other men so that those others ought to obey and may rightfully be made to obey them? On the one hand, it was argued that God had given to some men title to rule without the need of any consent. On the other hand, it was urged that title to govern was derived from the consent of the governed. The lawyer might hold either of these as a political doctrine and yet be so trained in the legal tradition and well read in the law books that he would insist upon the limitations on royal authority which had been established in the medieval charters and judicial decisions under them and on the legal responsibility of those purporting to exercise the powers of the king beyond those limits. This explains much that seems inconsistent in the course taken by some of the strongest lawyers of the time. Those who believed in divine right as a religious and political doctrine might be willing to concede a great deal to royal prerogative and yet, when it came to certain fundamentals, obviously guaranteed by Magna Carta and backed by the course of decision since the fourteenth century, might be firm in resistance to royal infringement of them. Thus Chief Justice Herbert, who held for the dispensing power and in 1688 followed James II to France, nevertheless refused a rule for execution of a soldier tried by a military tribunal without authority of Parliament. Likewise Sir Thomas Jones, who supported the crown in the proceedings against the City of London, refused to give James II an advance opinion in favor of a complete and absolute dispensing power. Except in cases in which it is not settled, the law as a taught tradition will hold judges in spite of political conviction, economic interest, or personal inclination.

Sir Edward Coke (pronounced Cook), solicitor general and then attorney general under Elizabeth, and Chief Justice of the Common Pleas and afterwards of the King's Bench under James I, is the great figure in the contests between the crown and the courts. He was educated at Trinity College, Cambridge and in law at the Inner Temple, and called to the bar in 1578. At the outset of his professional career, the same year, he succeeded on behalf of the defendant in an action for slander of a nobleman, one of the cases in which it was laid down that an act of Parliament against common right and reason is void. Even then his reputation for learning was so great that he was made a lecturer at one of the Inns within a year after his call. He was successively recorder of Coventry, recorder of Norwich, and recorder of London, and in 1592 solicitor general. In 1593 he was Speaker of the House of Commons, and in 1593 attorney general. As a law officer of the crown he had to take part in some state trials on the side of the crown in the days when procedure bore heavily against the accused and the ethics of advocacy on behalf of the prosecution were not what they afterwards became. He is much blamed to-day for what was usual in advocacy in crown cases at that time and has some parallel in sensational criminal trials in America.

On the bench all appearance of subserviency to the crown disappeared. He asserted judicial independence and opposed all attempts of the king to stretch his prerogative. As will be told more fully presently, he made it plain that the king had no personal judicial power. When he with the other judges were required to go before the council to justify a judgment, he protested against the growing practice of calling the judges to account in this way instead of reviewing the judgment for error in the due course of legal procedure. In 1610, in opposition to the council, he gave it as his opinion that the king could not create new criminal offenses by proclamation. In 1611, the Court of Common Pleas under his leadership discharged on habeas corpus a person imprisoned by warrant from the High Commission. Later when he was appointed to that commission he declined to serve.

As a writer on the common law, in spite of a quaint, often pedantic style, and complete lack of arrangement in his commentaries, he has the highest authority. His *First Institute,* or *Commentary on Littleton* (a treatise on tenures by a judge of the reign of Edward IV), his *Second Institute,* a commentary on Magna Carta and the old statutes of Edward I, his *Third Institute,* a treatise on pleas of the crown (i.e. criminal law), and his *Fourth Institute,* a treatise on the jurisdiction of courts, are books of authority, that is, they are binding authority of themselves, not depending on the authority of the statutes and decisions they cite. His reports of decisions of the courts while he was at the bar and on the bench had such authority that they were long, and by old-fashioned lawyers still are, cited as Reports, *simpliciter,* without the name of the reporter. He is universally regarded by lawyers as the oracle of the common law. No better champion of liberty secured by law could have been found.

His constant rival was Bacon. A great philosopher, Bacon was far from being Coke's equal as a lawyer. He was a courtier and a politician, stood consistently for absolute monarchy, and was in continual intrigue for political preferment, while Coke was a lawyer pure and simple. But Bacon's standing in letters and in philosophy have given him an advantage with the laity, who are apt to think of Coke as a narrow, pedantic lawyer who stood in the way of the great plans of an enlightened philosopher. Writers of the seventeenth century who reflect the ideas of the king and of the party strong for unlimited royal prerogative circulated many derogatory stories of his attitude towards the crown and his alleged subserviency. Partisans of Bacon depreciate him as Bacon's rival. This, of course, he could not be except as a lawyer. Ben Jonson's epigram upon him about the time of his removal from the bench and Milton's lines a generation later, together with the opinion of the profession then and ever since, tell more than the derogatory gossip dug up three centuries later, in another era of growing absolutism, and represented as the true Coke.

As to Coke's opposition to equity, we must remember what Selden, a great contemporary legal scholar, had to say of it. The chancellor who dispensed it was not necessarily a lawyer. He was and had to be a courtier and politician. He had to be a supporter of extreme claims of royal prerogative. Under James II to hold his place he had to become an apostate. The measure of his judicial action was his conscience, and, as Selden put it, might have been the length of his foot, for as one chancellor had a long foot and another a short foot and another an indifferent foot, so one might have a long conscience, and another a short conscience, and another an indifferent conscience. After Coke's time equity became systematized and was made part of the common-law system. But this process was not complete till Lord Eldon, chancellor almost continuously from 1801 to 1827. Two great American states would not receive it until its administration had been thoroughly subjected to principles.

One of the outstanding events of the contest beween the

crown and the courts was the conference between James I and the twelve judges of England in 1612. It appeared that the High Commission, an administrative tribunal established by Queen Elizabeth for the regulation of the church, had begun to take cognizance of temporal matters and deal with lay offenders. This tribunal was wholly unknown to common law and decided according to no fixed rules and subject to no appeal. When it sought to send its pursuivant to the house of a lay subject and arrest him upon a complaint of a wholly temporal nature, the Court of Common Pleas stopped the proceedings with a writ of prohibition—a common-law writ used where a court is proceeding beyond its jurisdiction. To meet this judicial insistence on the supremacy of law it was suggested by the Archbishop of Canterbury that the king might remove from the judges any cause he pleased and decide it in person; and the immediate business of the Sunday morning conference of judges was to explain this proposition and hear what the judges could say to it. The Archbishop of Canterbury expounded the alleged royal prerogative, saying that the judges were only the delegates of the king so that the king might do himself, when it seemed best to him, what he usually left to these delegates. The archbishop added that this was clear if not in law yet beyond question in divinity since it could be shown from the word of God in the Scriptures. To this Coke answered on behalf of the judges that by the law of England the king in person could not adjudge any cause. All cases, civil and criminal, were to be determined in some court of justice according to the law and custom of the realm. "But," said the king, "I thought law was founded upon reason, and I and others have reason as well as the judges." "True it was," Coke responded, "that God had endowed

His Majesty with excellent science and great endowments of nature; but His Majesty was not learned in the laws of his realm of England, and causes which concern the life or inheritance or goods or fortunes of his subjects are not to be decided by natural reason, but by the artificial reason and judgment of the law, which law is an art which requires long study and experience before that a man can attain to the cognizance of it." At this the king was greatly offended saying that in such case he should be under the law which it was treason to affirm. Coke answered in the words of Bracton, that the king ought not to be under any man, but under God and the law.

Coke was in error historically in saying that no king since the conquest had adjudged causes in person. Henry II had done so and had even put out of court a learned clerk who suggested arguments adverse to the judgment the king had determined to render. But the kings had long ceased to sit as judges and from the fourteenth century adjudication had been the exclusive province of the judges. Magna Carta called for the law of the land and that was something the king was not competent to administer.

After his removal from the bench, Coke sat in Parliament from 1621 to 1628 and was conspicuous in political opposition to James I and Charles I. He took a prominent part against royal monopolies, unlawful grants, and like abuses and was chairman of a committee to consider supply. He spoke strongly for a remonstrance and petition to the king, and stood boldly for the privileges of the House of Commons. The king proceeded highhandedly against the members who had opposed him. Coke was imprisoned, his papers were seized, and prosecutions were begun against him on trumped-up charges. He was in prison for seven months. In the new Parliament he was again active against the king's arbitrary measures. But James I died not long after. In the first Parliament of Charles I, Coke opposed grant of supply without a redress of grievances and urged a petition to the king according to the old precedents. The Parliament was dissolved, and in order to prevent the more independent members from sitting in the next one the king appointed them (Coke among others) sheriffs in the counties in which they lived. Coke was elected for another county, but did not sit. In the third Parliament of Charles I, however, at the age of 78, he took an active part, suggesting and succeeding in carrying the Petition of Right, which with Magna Carta, the Bill of Rights of 1688, the Declaration of Independence, and the Constitution of the United States stands as one of the monuments of Anglo-American free institutions. While he was on his deathbed in 1633, the manuscript of his *Second Institute* and all his papers were seized by direction of the king under pretense of search for seditious writings. Only the first eleven parts of his reports and the *First Institute* were published in his lifetime.

In 1642, Coke's *Second Institute*, containing his commentary on Magna Carta, was published by order of the House of Commons. This commentary was greatly relied upon in the controversies between the colonies and the British government before the Revolution and furnished much of the material for our American bills of rights. It is a foundation document for the history of our constitutional law. The part especially noteworthy is the long commentary on chapters 39 and 40 in which he takes them up clause by clause and shows how they have been interpreted and developed by legislation of Parliament, in the law books, and by judicial decision. He considers the meaning of *lex terrae,* "law of the land," and shows that as far back as the reign of Edward III the phrase "due process of law" was used as its equivalent. In other words, law in that phrase meant more than an aggregate of laws, and due process of law had much more than a merely procedural meaning. As these phrases were put in our American constitutions by lawyers who took the *Second Institute* for a legal Bible, this exposition needs to be remembered. Again, he shows the broad principle behind the provision as to disseising. No one is to be put out of his freehold or "put from his livelihood" except by a lawful proceeding of which he has full notice and in which he has full and fair hearing. He explains the word "liberties" as meaning more than freedom of the physical person from arrest or imprisonment. This meaning of liberty is of the first importance and he develops it fully and goes elaborately into the legal remedies. But he shows that it had always been construed to cover "the freedoms that men have." Thus in an old case an ordinance that every member of the merchant tailors' company should put half of his clothes to be dressed by some cloth worker, member of the same company, under penalty for not doing so, was held void as against the liberty of the subject who in common right and reason had a right to put his clothes to be dressed by whom he pleased. Those who have been arguing recently that the word "liberty" in our constitutions refers only to freedom from external restraint of the physical person need to note that the word was used by the framers of our constitutions in the sense in which they found it used in the law books from which they got their ideas of the guaranteed rights of Englishmen as natural rights of men. Coke points out that monopolies and impositions upon trade without authority of law come under the ban of deprivation of liberty.

Other features of importance for American constitutional law are the discussion of searches and seizures in connection with the clause in Magna Carta that the king would not "send upon" a free man; the exposition of "taken or imprisoned," of "destroyed," of "judgment of his peers," and of "lawful judgment." Here he considers the necessity of giving one whose rights are to be affected by official action a full and fair opportunity to meet the case against him—something we have been forgetting in much summary administrative action nowadays. His discussion of the clause as to denying or delaying justice is important also. The citizens of Boston relied on it when the courts were closed under the Stamp Act. Finally, the discussion of the law of the land as the birthright of Englishmen was made good use of in the contests with the British government which led to the Revolution.

After Coke's death came the famous case of ship money. The king claimed a prerogative of assessing on seaports a contribution towards providing and equipping ships of war to guard against pirates and dangers involved in war. As Parliament would vote no supply until grievances were redressed, the king's advisers hit upon the idea of extending the writs for ship money to the whole kingdom. The sheriffs were directed to assess every landholder and other inhabitant according to their judgment of his means. Hampden, whose assessment amounted to only twenty shillings, refused to pay and the matter came into court. On account of its importance the case was heard before all the judges in the Exchequer Chamber. Seven of the twelve judges gave judgment for the crown. The Chief Justice of the King's Bench and the Chief Baron of the Exchequer held for Hampden on technical grounds, although agreeing with the majority on the substantive question that the king could on his own allegation of public danger require an inland county to furnish ships or money by way of commutation for defense of the coast. Another judge gave a short written opinion in favor of Hampden. Croke and Hutton, two judges of reputation and experience, boldly pronounced against the claim of the crown. An act of Parliament in 1641 invalidated all the proceedings and declared against the asserted prerogative.

Meanwhile the courts, after the medieval precedents, were enforcing the medieval fundamental law against Parliament. The first case of this sort after the Prior of Castleacre's Case was Lord Cromwell's Case in 1578, Coke's first important case as counsel. The action was brought by a peer against a clergyman for slander in saying that the lord liked those who maintained sedition against the queen's proceedings. After the defendant's plea of justification had been held insufficient, Coke moved in arrest of judgment on the ground that the plaintiff's declaration, i.e. statement of his cause of action, was bad for not properly reciting the statute of Richard II on which the action was brought. If the statute was a public act the court would take judicial notice of it and the misrecital would not matter. If it was a private act it had to be pleaded and the court could only go by the record before it. But taking it as it was pleaded, the act was void because against law, that is, the law of the land, or as Coke expounds more fully in the *Second Institute,* common right and reason. As it stood it had the effect of punishing those who had not offended. On this basis nineteenth-century American courts at one time held statutes imposing liability upon those not at fault to be wanting in due process of law.

Next, in 1610, came Bonham's Case, in which Coke sat as chief justice. Here an act of Parliament, confirming the charter of the Royal College of Physicians, gave the incorporated society of physicians power to impose fines upon physicians offending against its rules, the fines to be payable half to the crown and half to the society. Dr. Bonham, having been imprisoned for nonpayment of a fine imposed under this provision, brought an action for false imprisonment. The Court of King's Bench held the imprisonment wrongful on two grounds: (1.) that the charter, confirmed by the statute, did not extend the jurisdiction of the College of Physicians beyond those practicing in London, and (2.) that the statute which made the college, which got half of the fine, judge of its own case, complainant, prosecutor, and judge, was against common right and reason and void. The court cited on this last proposition the cases as to seals of ecclesiastical corporations discussed in the first lecture, and a case in the reign of Elizabeth in which a statute in general terms was held not to be so construed as to reach a result contrary to due process of law. But Bonham's Case did not involve a mere matter of interpretation. The question was whether Parliament could validly enact that one should be both judge and party—judge in his own case.

In 1615, the question came up again in the Common Pleas in the case of Day v. Savadge. Here the authorities of the City of London seized a bag of nutmegs, deposited on a wharf belonging to the city, to be transported by water, claiming a customary charge due the city. To this the plaintiff, suing in trespass, pleaded an immemorial custom that freemen of the city (i.e. members of the corporation) were not subject to the charge, and alleged that he was a freeman of the city. The defendant denied the alleged custom and claimed the benefit of an act of Parliament that when a custom of London was in issue the court should apply to the mayor and aldermen of the city to certify what the custom was. The court held that it was "against right and justice and against natural equity" to allow the mayor and eldermen to try and judge their own case by their own certificate. The court said that even an act of Parliament to make a man judge in his own case was "void in itself."

One of the clear prerogatives of the crown, the extent and limits of which were not clear, was that of dispensing with the operation of a particular law in a particular case for great hardship. As far back as the Anglo-Saxon laws it was laid down that if "the law was too heavy" one was to apply to the king. This royal authority had become the basis of equity jurisdiction of the Chancellor. But an undefined part remained in the king. James II, wishing to appoint Catholics to commands in the army, appointed Sir Edward Hales colonel of a regiment with a dispensation under the great seal to act notwithstanding the statute requiring all office-holders to take an oath and receive the sacrament according to the rites of the Church of England. An action of debt was brought for the penalty prescribed by the statute, and the defendant having pleaded the dispensation, the plaintiff demurred. The case, brought in the King's Bench, was argued before the twelve judges of England, and eleven gave judgment for the defendant on the ground that to dispense with penal laws for necessary and urgent reasons was "an inseparable prerogative of the king," and that "no act of Parliament could take away that power." The whole dispensing power was abrogated at the Revolution of 1688.

Again in 1695, in King v. Earl of Banbury, Lord Holt,

one of the great judges in English judicial history, said *arguendo* that the courts could adjudge acts of Parliament to be void, and the question came squarely before him on a writ of error in a case brought from the Mayor's Court in City of London v. Wood in 1701. The action was debt to recover for a forfeiture to the city under a bylaw of the city by virtue of an act of Parliament. It was held that the action could not be brought in the Court of the Mayor and Aldermen by the mayor and aldermen on behalf of the mayor and aldermen, the very persons who were to have the benefit of the forfeiture being judges in their own case. One of the judges cited Day v. Savadge and Lord Holt cited and approved Bonham's Case.

What was the fundamental law which the courts considered violated by the acts of Parliament in these cases? In Day v. Savadge, Chief Justice Hobart spoke of natural law, the ideal law of which we heard much in this country in the eighteenth century and in our formative era before the Civil War. But the English lawyers had always preferred to speak of "the law of reason." What Coke speaks of as "common right and reason" was what was meant. The law of the land, declared by Magna Carta, forbade arbitrary and unreasonable governmental action, such as to punish the innocent and to make one a judge in his own case. This idea came into our bills of rights in the provisions against deprivation of life, liberty, or property without due process of law. Due process of law meant according to the law of the land.

In King v. Earl of Banbury and City of London v. Wood, Lord Holt had not perceived that the effect of the English Revolution had been to set up a parliamentary absolutism after the attempt to set up a royal absolutism had failed. Coke had been troubled between a claim of absolute sovereignty in Parliament and the medieval precedents he followed in Bonham's Case. Blackstone was not clear about it in 1765. The present English doctrine was not thoroughly received till the nineteenth century. Much logical acrobatics has been indulged in in order to push the present English doctrine back into the medieval cases. There is no need of this. The Revolution of 1688 made a profound change in the English constitution. The seventeenth-century polity as set forth in Coke's doctrine was the one we accepted at our Revolution and put in our constitutions. When these instruments declare themselves the "supreme law of the land" they use the language of Magna Carta as interpreted by Coke.

The history of constitutional guarantees of liberty in England culminates in the Bill of Rights of 1688. We have next to turn to the history of such guarantees in the American colonies.

3

In the American Colonies

IN THE AMERICAN COLONIES in the eighteenth century
a situation arose quite parallel to that which existed
during the contests between the crown and the courts in
seventeenth-century England. In England the prerogatives of the crown were not clearly defined. Wide claims
could be made for them and equally strong claims could
be made for limitations on them. A body of absolute political doctrine as to the powers of rulers had grown up on the
Continent, and the two countries which then set the
fashion in politics, France and Spain, were autocratic
monarchies. On the other hand, the English lawyers had
received a taught tradition of limitations on governmental
action, subjection of officials to the law of the land, and
rights guaranteed by law to the subject. In America, a
rapidly developing country, with expanding trade and
commerce, with great natural wealth, with an adventurous pioneer population, with its own legislatures and
courts, found itself politically thirteen distinct provinces,
each subject to absolute government from Westminster.
The legal incidents of the relation between the British
government and the colonies were not clearly defined.
There had been no need of defining them. In the era of
colonization the settlements had been feeble, had needed
the protection of the home government, and had raised
no questions as to its powers. But the home government

in the eighteenth century, like the English king in the seventeenth century, needed money badly and was looking for sources of revenue. As the king sought to raise money by impositions by his own authority, without the consent of Parliament representing the people who were to pay, so the home government sought to raise money from the colonies without applying to them or obtaining their consent. Moreover, the regime of absolute monarchy at which the Stuarts aimed involved the disregard of individual interests which had long been recognized and restriction on individual activity and enterprise, which inevitably met with resistance in a time of faith in individual reason, breakdown of authoritarianism, and restless, acquisitive self-assertion. In colonial America of the eighteenth century the completely centralized government, through the Board of Trade and Plantations, the Privy Council, and Parliament, with no consciousness of limitations beyond what Mr. Dooley called gentlemanly restraint, involved like disregard of recognized individual interests and restrictions on individual activity and enterprise. People who had cleared the wilderness, fought with the savages, and established flourishing centers of trade and commerce in the new world did not take kindly to the restraints which the colonial status was held to involve.

Lawyers played a chief part in the contests with the Stuarts. They found their weapons in the doctrines which had been worked out by the experience of the common-law courts in trying official action by the provisions of the Great Charter. Coke made the cases under the Plantagenets the material for a commentary on Magna Carta which made a treaty between the paramount landlord and his tenants in chief a legal document defining limitations in the relation of ruler and ruled. What the medieval cases and tradition were to Coke, Coke's *Second Institute* and the decisions of the common-law courts he discusses or that followed him were to the American lawyers before the Revolution. In each case the opposition was both legal and political. Lawyers took part in each in both capacities. But the lawyers gave a legal turn to the political opposition, and the result was a nation ruled by law and on this side of the water a written constitution as fundamental law carrying on the medieval English idea of the law of the land.

So steeped were the eighteenth-century colonial lawyers in Coke's teachings, for Coke's *Institutes* were the most authoritative law books available to them and they were dealing with a tradition, not a code, that the controversial literature of the era of the Revolution, if it is to be understood, must be read or interpreted by a common-law lawyer. Indeed, he must be a common-law lawyer of the nineteenth-century type, brought up to read and reread Coke and Blackstone till he got the whole feeling and atmosphere of those who led resistance to the home government. It was a wrench to many a Cavalier lawyer, whose father had fought for Charles I, to stand for the law of the land against James II. It was a wrench for many a loyal Englishman in the colonies, trained in law in one of the Inns of Court, to take a stand which branded him as a rebel because he held to the teachings of his law books and felt bound to resist the claim of the British government to absolute rule.

While according to American legal theory the colonists brought the common law of England with them when they came to the New World, there was for some time no need of so advanced and technical a body of legal precepts as the seventeenth-century English law. Law, as distinguished from laws, requires lawyers, and law and lawyers are little needed until there is a considerable economic development. A frontier society needs little more than offhand magisterial justice. For example, the beginnings of the administration of justice in New England were by no means legal justice. An English lawyer who came to Boston about 1637 wrote in 1642 that the colonial tribunals ignored the English common law and sought to administer the Mosaic law. The laws in seventeenth-century England were hard on the dissenters who were largely colonizing America, and the experience of administration of justice which many of them had had was one of highhanded enforcement of penal statutes by magistrates. Accordingly, they were inclined to assume that law was "a dark and knavish business." Where the layman in the colonies at that time knew something about law he was likely to find that its ideals were those of the relationally organized society of the Middle Ages and so out of touch with those of the pioneers who were opening up the wilderness.

Need for law and for lawyers came with the economic development of the colonies and the rise of trade and commerce. From the beginning there had been colonial legislation, subject to disallowance for not conforming to the common law or to English legislation, and so calling for some knowledge of English law by those who drafted it. Appeals to the Privy Council required more care on the part of court and counsel and parties since the expense of taking a case to Westminster and the delay and expense in defending a judgment there were serious. In the latter part of the seventeenth century a system of courts replaced legislative justice and magistrates, and at the end of the century the courts of review began to be manned by trained lawyers. Moreover, at the same time and in the

eighteenth century there came to be an increasing number of lawyers in the colonies who had been trained in
the Inns of Court.

In Pennsylvania, Andrew Hamilton, a barrister and
bencher of Gray's Inn, came to Philadelphia in 1682. He
is well known for his defense of Zenger in 1735, the pioneer case of freedom of the press, in which he argued suc-
cessfully for the common-law rights of Englishmen. In the
time just before the Revolution five barristers of the
Middle Temple were at the Pennsylvania bar, and two
of them signed the Declaration of Independence.

In Virginia, William Fitzhugh, educated as a lawyer in
England, was practicing in 1680. In the first half of the
eighteenth century there were six who had been trained
in the Inns of Court, three of them becoming attorneys
general. The leader of these was Sir John Randolph, who
at his death in 1737 was counted among the conspicuous
leaders of the profession in America. Between 1750 and
the Revolution there was an exceptionally strong group
of lawyers in Virginia, many of them trained in the Inns
of Court, and others taught by those so trained, among
them George Wythe, who afterwards decided one of the
pioneer cases refusing to give effect to a legislative order
contrary to the state constitution, and George Mason, who
drafted the first American bill of rights.

In Maryland, Daniel Dulany, Sr., a barrister of Gray's
Inn, was admitted to the bar of the Provincial Court in
1710. One of the first items in the events that led to the
Revolution is his pamphlet, *The Right of the Inhabitants
of Maryland to the Benefit of English Laws* (1728), growing out of disallowance of provincial legislation by the
proprietor. Daniel Dulany, Jr., also trained in the Inns of
Court, admitted in 1747, was the leader of the bar in

struggles over arbitrary assertions of legislative powers by royal governors and in the agitation over the Stamp Act. His pamphlet, *Considerations on the Propriety of Imposing Taxes on the British Colonies for the Purpose of Raising a Revenue by Act of Parliament* (1765), is one of the classics of that controversy. Four Maryland lawyers who signed the Declaration of Independence had studied law in the Inns of Court.

In Massachusetts in 1647 the governor and assistants ordered the importation, among other books, of two copies each of Coke's *First* and *Second Institute* and of Coke's Reports. This was said to be done "to the end that we may have better light for making and proceeding about laws." But the leaders of the bar who took part in the agitation over the Stamp Act and the events that led to the Revolution were not educated in the Inns of Court. Nor were the lawyers of colonial New York who resisted the attempt of the royal governor to review verdicts of the jury on the facts. But their reading of the law books made them obnoxious to the governor, who wrote to Lord Halifax that they enlarged the popular side of government and depreciated the powers of the crown.

Of the signers of the Declaration of Independence from North Carolina, both were lawyers, one of whom had studied under James Otis and the other under Edward Pendleton. Thus both were well grounded in Coke's doctrines. Three of the lawyers practicing in the province before the Revolution were trained in England.

In South Carolina thirteen of the lawyers at the bar before the Revolution had studied in the Inns of Court. The leader among them was John Rutledge, barrister of the Inner Temple in 1761, foremost in opposition to the Stamp Act.

It will have been seen that lawyers trained in the Inns of Court and those who had studied in their offices in America took an active part in the contests which led to the Revolution. But where there were no lawyers trained in the Inns of Court, lawyers who had "read law" had read Coke's *Institutes*, published between 1628 and 1644, the authoritative systematic exposition of the common law down to Blackstone's *Commentaries*, published 1765–69. Thus they were brought up on ideas of "the law of the land," of the immemorial rights of Englishmen guaranteed by Magna Carta. Blackstone at once became the first book to be studied by American lawyers and held that place till the beginning of the present century. The *Commentaries* had an exceptionally large sale in the colonies. We are told that twenty-five hundred copies were bought in America before the Revolution. A subscription reprint was published in Philadelphia in 1771–72, and the list of subscribers is headed by "John Adams, Esq. barrister at law, Boston, Massachusetts Bay." Blackstone set forth Coke's doctrine in readable form.

Five ideas were assumed by American lawyers of the time of the Revolution, and by our lawyers of the nineteenth century, as involved in government according to law in contrast to absolute monarchy. They were: (1.) the idea of a fundamental law, the "law of the land," to which all official and governmental action was bound to conform, which law was to be applied by the courts in the course of orderly litigation according to the common law, and could be invoked against officials by anyone aggrieved; (2.) the idea of immemorial rights of Englishmen, secured by the law of the land, and of the common law in which they were recognized as the birthright of Englishmen and so of Americans. Coke's *Second Institute* speaks of the law of the land as the "best inheritance that the subject hath" and is full of old law-French maxims expressing that idea; (3.) the idea of authoritative declarations of these rights in charters and bills of rights. Indeed, there was a precedent for a written constitution, such as all Americans believed in after independence, in the Instrument of Government adopted under the Commonwealth in 1653. It contained a few declarations of fundamental rights and provided "that all laws, statutes, ordinances, and clauses in any law statute and ordinance, to the contrary of the aforesaid liberty shall be esteemed null and void"; (4.) the idea of an independent judiciary, as set forth in the English Bill of Rights of 1688, to administer the fundamental law, and of lawmaking by a body distinct from the executive; (5.) the idea of courts refusing to apply statutes in contravention of the fundamental law: an idea made familiar not only by the seventeenth-century cases which the lawyers found in the abridgments or digests of reported decisions and reports, but also by appeals to the Privy Council in which statutes were held to conflict with colonial charters or to run counter to provisions in charters for legislation in accordance with or not repugnant to the common law.

In 1687, the first American law book was published in Philadelphia. Its title is as significant as its contents. The title page reads:

> The Excellent Priviledge of Liberty & Property, being the Birthright of the Free-born Subjects of England. Containing I Magna Charta, with a learned Comment upon it. II The Confirmation of the Charters of the Liberties of England and of the Forrest, made in the 35th year of Edward the First. III A Statute made the 34 Edw. I commonly called De Tallageo non Conce-

dendo; wherein all Fundamental Laws, Liberties and Customs are confirmed. With a Comment upon it. IV An abstract of the Pattent granted by the King to William Penn and his Heirs and Assigns for the Province of Pennsilvania. V and Lastly, the Charter of Liberties granted by the said William Penn to the Free-men and Inhabitants of the Province of Pennsilvania and Territories thereto annexed, in America.

There is a Latin motto to the effect that a greater inheritance comes to each of us from law and laws than from parents. The commentary is taken from Coke's *Second Institute*. In 1721 a book was published in Boston entitled *English Liberties or the Freeborn Subject's Inheritance*. It contains, among other things, Magna Carta, the confirmatory statute of Edward I, the Habeas Corpus Act, a Declaration of the Liberties of the Subject, and the Petition of Right. Coke's *Second Institute* is drawn on extensively. The law books of the time commonly repeat out of Coke's commentary a law-French saying of the Middle Ages that the "law is the greatest inheritance the king hath, for without the law there would be no king and no inheritance." It should be added that on the eve of the Revolution in 1774, in a case of Campbell v. Hall in the King's Bench, an action to recover from the king's collector of customs a duty imposed by royal proclamation upon sugar exported from the island of Grenada, the court, in an opinion by Lord Mansfield, one of the greatest of common-law judges, rendered judgment for the plaintiff, holding that where a local legislature had been set up, the pre-existing law of the island could only be changed by that legislature or by Parliament. Thus while American lawyers were urging restrictions of fundamental law which forbade impositions upon the colonies without their consent, the law of the land was being enforced against the crown and its officers in the nearby Caribbean. This could but confirm American lawyers in their belief in a fundamental law.

Legislation in South Carolina in 1712 adopted as the law of that province "all such statutes in the kingdom of England as declare the rights and liberties of the subjects and enact the better securing of the same," and "such parts of statutes as declare the rights and liberties of subjects." Such statutes, aimed at the royal governors, grew out of friction between the lawyers, arguing for restrictions resting on fundamental law, and the absentee government by authority of the crown. They asserted the immemorial rights of Englishmen. The tract of Daniel Dulany, Sr. in 1728, Andrew Hamilton's argument at the trial of Zenger (1735), Otis' argument against writs of assistance (1761), the tract of the younger Daniel Dulany against the Stamp Act (1765), and the Declaration of Rights of the Continental Congress (1774) all insist upon the common-law rights of Englishmen as the rights of the colonists. It is worth while to quote from the latter: "That our ancestors who first settled these colonies were, at the time of their emigration from the mother country, entitled to all the rights, liberties and immunities of free and natural born subjects within the realm of England." John Adams in 1765 argued that the Stamp Act was "utterly void," (1.) as contrary to the natural rights of man, and (2.) as contrary to the liberties of Englishmen. It should be noted here how a philosophical political idea and a historical legal idea are fusing in the argument of one who perhaps was more politician than lawyer. It will be necessary to speak more fully of this fusion in another connection. The Continental Congress made its claims in title of "the immutable laws of nature, the principles of the English constitution, and the several charters of compacts." But it asserts them as Englishmen.

It may well be asked at this point, why did none of these charters of liberties and no declaration of rights down to the Virginia Bill of Rights of 1776 include freedom of writing and speaking and freedom of the press, which now stand first in our national Bill of Rights and in bills of rights generally in the states?

It is not difficult to understand why nothing was said on this subject in the Constitution of the United States as first adopted. The men who were framing that Constitution were chiefly interested in a frame of government to supersede the old Articles of Confederation. George Mason, who drew the Virginia Bill of Rights, did urge one for the federal Constitution, but little attention was paid to him. It was considered that each state had a bill of rights, needed because of the plenary lawmaking power of the states. But the powers of the federal government were only those given it by the Constitution, and it was thought that power to do the things feared and guarded against by bills of rights had not been given to the general government. However, people generally in the country feared that the new government they had set up over their local governments would do the things the British government had done, and insisted on the first nine amendments. The two things in the bills of rights that are not in Coke's *Second Institute* are freedom of the press and freedom of religion, and the reason is historical.

Today the Supreme Court of the United States holds that the provisions in the First Amendment as to freedom of speech and of the press and freedom of religion are included in the Fourteenth Amendment; that they are to be deduced from the idea of liberty which is secured against the states by that amendment. That is the logical deduction from the idea of liberty as Coke defines it. Coke could very well have argued for these things in his Commentary on Magna Carta. Why didn't he? The reason is historical. In the seventeenth century the common-law courts and lawyers had not been confronted with these questions. In his day they were in the jurisdiction of the Star Chamber, not of the courts. In the Middle Ages the king was in a pretty constant struggle with the feudal nobility as to who was to hold the reins of government. Before and after the Reformation there was long a struggle between state and church whether there was to be a political organization of society or a religious organization. Thus the dignity of the political authorities was a very important consideration. Anyone who criticized the government was weakening the power of the government in these struggles. The government in consequence was very jealous of any criticism of any sort. Such cases were dealt with in the Star Chamber, in which common-law judges sat with others and no doubt operated in some measure as a check. But that tribunal was an administrative agency. If one criticized the government so as to endanger its supremacy or interfere with its efficient functioning, he was brought up before and disciplined by the Star Chamber. The consequence was that there are no discussions of freedom of speaking (except in Parliament) and freedom of religious belief in the *Second Institute*.

But there came to be every reason in the eighteenth century why the colonies should be concerned about freedom of speech and of the press as they began to be irked by the complete centralization of power at Westminster and by the highhanded methods of royal governors. The pamphlets published by leading lawyers against the Stamp Act, the pamphlets attacking the disallowance of colonial statutes by the Privy Council, the legal arguments against arbitrary conduct of royal governors were considered seditious by the home government and the governors. But juries commonly thought otherwise, so that there was a continual contest to get these matters away from juries and before appointees of and dependents upon the government.

After the Star Chamber was abolished, Charles II attempted to use the courts by orders in the nature of an injunction against publication of matter obnoxious to the government. Chief Justice Scroggs was impeached in 1681 among other things for such an order, but escaped by dissolution of Parliament. The method of dealing with such cases which remained was called an information *ex officio* brought by the attorney general for a seditious libel. A seditious libel for the purposes of this proceeding was a publication which the government did not like. It might criticize the conduct of the government or of some particular official. If Parliament was criticized, or some member of Parliament, the House of Commons took it up. Between the Restoration (1660) and the Revolution, there were no less than forty-two cases of imprisonment by order of the House of Commons for criticizing Parliament or some member of Parliament. But if the crown was criticized, or the ministers of the crown, resort was had to information ex officio by the attorney general.

What this signified was that it did not require indictment by a grand jury. In an ordinary case of a serious crime there had to be an indictment or presentment by a grand jury. But if the king or the ministers of the king were criticized the attorney general filed an information

ex officio on which the accused could be tried. The difficulty in these cases was to get juries to convict. The sheriff
was appointed by the crown and removed by the crown,
and he picked the jury. For example, in the trial of the
Seven Bishops for presenting a statement to James II as
to his illegal Declaration of Indulgence, the king's brewer
was on the jury. He is reported to have said that if he
found the bishops guilty he could sell no more beer to
the people, while if he found them not guilty he could
sell no more to the king. One need not say that the latter
alternative was the reason the sheriff put him on the
jury.

Of the English cases which attracted particular attention between the reign of James II and the adoption of
our federal Constitution there are ten which stand out.
The political literature of the time is full of discussion of
them. It is enough to mention here the case of John
Wilkes in 1765, the cases of Almon, Miller, and Woodfall,
who published the letter of Junius to the king (1770), and
the case of the dean of St. Asaph's in 1783. The dean of St.
Asaph's procured the publication of a document called
A Dialogue between a Scholar and a Farmer, written by a
barrister, which severely criticized the contemporary situation in British politics. Accordingly, an information ex
officio was filed and the dean was tried in the Court of
King's Bench. The chief justice, following the law which
had been laid down in the time of the Stuarts, charged the
jury that it was for the court and not the jury to say what
was a seditious libel: all that the jury could try was
whether it had been published or procured to be published by the accused. But the jury in many of these cases,
as in the Case of the Seven Bishops, took advantage of its

power to render a general verdict of acquittal, in spite of the charge of the court.

Such was the situation in eighteenth-century England. Much the same story is to be told for the colonies. The first newspaper published in this country, published in 1690, was suppressed after the first issue because it indulged in reflections on the colonial government. The second was subjected to a censorship, the censors being appointed by the royal governor. Censorship was abolished in England in the reign of William III, but it continued in the colonies. It was an institution of the church in the Middle Ages very proper possibly as to books on matters spiritual, but carried over into matters temporal, particularly matters political, open to grave objections. To pass, however, to the legal side of the matter, the case which immediately excited the public mind was that of John Peter Zenger in New York in 1734.

One Cosby was appointed governor of New York by the crown in 1734. He reached New York in August of that year, having had a long voyage. In the interval between his appointment and his arrival a certain Van Dam did the things to be done by the governor for which fees were chargeable, and collected the emoluments of the office. Governor Cosby claimed the money as belonging to him by virtue of his office from the date of his appointment, while Van Dam claimed a setoff for his work in performing the duties. The governor found that the local juries were not going to be favorable to him so he conceived the idea of setting up an equity jurisdiction in the Supreme Court. He had the power of appointing and removing judges and he removed the chief justice after the manner of a Stuart king because the judge's view of the law did not meet the governor's wishes. When Van Dam tried to bring a separate action to assert his claim he found that he could not get process served because the governor had the appointment and removal of those who alone could serve writs. Between 1701 and 1728 the legislature had refused repeatedly to set up a court of equity which could proceed without a jury. The Privy Council could reject any measure for better organization of courts that did not provide for a court of equity, but it could not compel the provincial legislature to establish one. An impasse resulted. So Governor Cosby set up a court of equity on his own responsibility, with no authority from anyone but himself, and his case against Van Dam was heard in that court. In truth, that court had no jurisdiction on principles of equity. The governor's claim called for an ordinary action at law for money had and received. But such things did not trouble a masterful royal governor of the eighteenth century.

Zenger was publishing a newspaper in New York after 1733. When Governor Cosby came, Zenger began to comment on his highhanded actions. He set up a censorship by his own authority and Zenger in a vigorous article on liberty of the press called attention to the way it operated under the control of the governor. In another article on the right of trial by jury he commented on the way the governor had tried to evade jury trial. At the governor's instance one of the justices of the Supreme Court charged the grand jury in strong terms about seditious libel, but the grand jury refused to indict Zenger. However, the sheriff was under the control of the governor and the sheriff picked the grand jury, so at the next term the chief justice charged the grand jury violently about seditious libel and Zenger was indicted.

Andrew Hamilton, one of the great lawyers of that time, came on from Philadelphia and defended. In those days one could argue law as well as facts to the jury, at least in a criminal case. He made a powerful argument based on Magna Carta, the law of the land, and the liberty of the subject, and Zenger was acquitted. The case attracted much attention throughout the country and was continually referred to in the discussions as to seditious libel which went on in England as well as America. The situation in which nobody could criticize the operations of government nor even comment on them was felt to be intolerable. This is the immediate background of the provision as to freedom of speech and of the press in all American bills of rights. The mischief was that the government had complete control over everything in the way of comment upon its operations. The remedy was to free expression of opinion, either in speech or in writing, from any restrictions imposed by the government.

Eight grievances which American lawyers regarded as violations of immemorial rights or liberties secured by the law of the land, as they found them declared in their law books, were: (1.) the imposition of taxes on and raising of revenue from the colonies without the consent of the legislative body representing them; (2.) the unification of all powers of government of the colonies in a centralized administration at Westminster which continually neglected or even positively injured the interests of the colonists in the interest of those who had influence on British politics; (3.) deprivation of jury trial by extending admiralty jurisdiction at the expense of the common law; (4.) providing for trials away from the vicinage so as to put parties to expense and annoyance and deprive them of the advantage of good repute among their neighbors; (5.) infringement of the right to assemble in order to consider grievances and petition the king for redress; (6.) quartering soldiers and keeping a standing army in time of peace without getting the consent of the colonial legislature. This was complained of specially in New England and echoes of the complaint may be seen in the bills of rights in Massachusetts and New Hampshire. It was a method of coercion attempted by James II and was expressly pronounced unlawful in the English bill of rights; (7.) requiring oppressive security from a claimant of seized property before he could claim it and defend his property rights. This practice, which reminds one of the methods of Empson and Dudley denounced by Coke as against the law of the land, was resorted to in enforcing the Navigation Acts by which the British government sought control of the trade and commerce of the colonies, requiring exports by way of England or in English ships and imports from or by way of England and in English ships; (8.) referring to those laws and to instructions to the royal governors as to industries in the colonies, interference with merchants and traders not in time of war, contrary to the interests of the colonies and without any reference to colonial legislatures.

As to the first, Otis put the matter thus: "Taxes are not to be laid on the people but by their consent in person or by deputy," and cites the *Second Institute* on impositions "laid by the king's absolute power." Also in arguing that subjects cannot lawfully be charged for the defense of the realm without their consent through their representatives he cites cases from the *Second Institute*. As to interference with the trade and commerce of the colonies, in his tract *The Rights of the American Colonies* he argues from Coke's *Second Institute,* the commentary on chapter 41 of Magna Carta. The first half of his argument in that tract is based on natural law and natural rights. The second half of his argument proceeds on Coke's *Second Institute*. In the instructions to the agent for Massachusetts by a committee of which Otis was a member, published as an appendix to his tract, it is said: "The judges of England have decided in favor of these sentiments when they expressly declare that . . . acts against the fundamental principles of the British Constitution are void." He cites Day v. Savadge, City of London v. Wood, and Bonham's Case, and a remark of Powys *arguendo* in a case in 1712 which, he shows, concedes the doctrine. If many of the American lawyers who cited those cases with assurance for a century after 1688 were trained in the Inns of Court in the eighteenth century, it only shows what one may see in the English reports of the time and in the doubtful language of Blackstone in 1765, that the English lawyers of the fore part of that century who were their teachers had not yet learned what the effect of the English Revolution was to be upon that part of the doctrine they had learned from the century before.

Even before the Revolution, along with the legal theory of the rights of Englishmen, defined by the law of the land and to be given effect by the common-law courts, a philosophical theory of natural rights of man, demonstrated by reason and morally binding on all rulers, began to be urged in America. In 1725, Gridley, the father of the Boston bar, advised John Adams that study of natural, i.e. ideal, law, set forth in the Continental treatises on the law of nature and nations, if unnecessary in England, was important for the American lawyer. After the break with authority at the Reformation, when jurists sought to find some unchallengeable basis for the binding force of law, they turned to reason. The Renaissance had brought in a boundless faith in reason. Where the Middle Ages had found a twofold foundation for truth in revelation and in reason, Grotius in 1625 had pronounced that he could conceive of natural law even if there were no God. In the philosophical jurisprudence of the eighteenth century the idea of natural law was universally accepted. Out of this theory of a universal ideal law grew a theory of natural, that is, ideal, rights, demonstrated by reason as deductions from human nature—from the ideal abstract man. Grotius defined a right as the moral quality which made it just and right that a man have certain things or do certain things. Contemporary jurists on the Continent held to four propositions: (1.) There are natural rights demonstrable by reason. They are eternal and absolute. They are valid for all men in all times and all places. (2.) Natural law is a body of rules, ascertainable by reason, which perfectly secures all these natural rights. (3.) The state exists only to secure men in these natural rights. (4.) Positive law, the law applied and enforced in the courts, is the means by which the state performs this function and is morally binding only so far as it conforms to natural law.

English lawyers have never had much concern with philosophy and natural law found little place in their books. Chief Justice Hobart in Day v. Savadge pronounced an act of Parliament making a man a judge in his own case, contrary both to the law of the land and to natural law, void in law and in morals. Blackstone set forth the theories of Grotius and announced the invalidity of positive laws at variance with natural law, but then set forth the immemorial common-law rights of Englishmen and explained that positive laws contrary to natural law were not binding in *foro conscientiae*. When Americans were beginning to think of independence the transition from the common-law rights of Englishmen, claimed in the Declaration of Rights of the Continental Congress in 1774, to the natural rights of man, claimed in the Declaration of Independence, was an easy one. It is significant that the rights claimed by either title were the same. John Adams, in *Novanglus*, argued that New Englanders derived their laws not from Parliament nor from the common law but from nature. Jefferson claimed the rights of Americans by the universal title of humanity when the breach with England made it awkward to claim them as Englishmen.

Down to the Declaration of Independence, however, the rights claimed are those of Englishmen. The memorial of the city of Boston, when the courts were closed because of the Stamp Act, claims the law as the best birthright of Englishmen. The Declaration of Rights of the Continental Congress claims the rights secured by royal charters and the benefit of the common law. The colonists were asserting something more than moral claims. Theirs were moral claims backed by the law of the land enforceable in the courts.

Moreover, as shown by the prologue to the Declaration of 1774, these rights had always been claimed and set forth in authoritative declarations: Magna Carta and its successive reissues; the Confirmation by Edward I; the Petition of Right; the English Bill of Rights. The words of the Declaration deserve to be quoted:

Whereupon the Deputies so appointed being now assembled in a full and free representation of these colonies, taking into their most serious consideration the

best means of attaining the ends aforesaid, do in the
first place, as Englishmen, their ancestors, in like cases
have usually done, for asserting and vindicating their
rights and liberties declare their claim to the legal
rights of free natural born subjects, to the common law,
to trial by jury, and to assemble peaceably to consider
grievances and petition for redress.

This language goes back to the Articles of the Barons, to
the Petition of Right, and to the English Bill of Rights.

As the Englishman at home objected to concentration
of all political power in the king, so the Englishman in
the colonies objected to concentration of all political
power over the colonies in the government at Westminster.
All acts of colonial legislatures were subject to veto by
the Privy Council. They could be "disallowed" within
five years, and even if not disallowed, when judgments
based on them came to be taken to the Privy Council on
appeal they might be held invalid as not in accord with
the common law or as in conflict with the colonial or provincial charter. Executive power was in the hands of a
governor appointed by the crown. The Board of Trade and
Plantations at Westminster sent him full instructions and
required reports from him to show that he was carrying
them out. The judges in the colonial courts were appointed
by the governor and removed by him. In Maryland, says
the historian of the courts, "The Governor had complete
control over the tenure of office of judges, all holding
office at his pleasure, and they came by reason of that fact
to be spoken of sometimes as 'minions of power' or 'satel-
lites.' " The governor's council, appointed by the crown
and holding during the pleasure of the crown, was the

upper house of the legislature. It was sometimes the court of equity with wide, ill-defined powers. It was sometimes the ultimate court of review subject to appeal to the Privy Council. What such a polity could mean is illustrated by Zenger's Case. It was properly objected to in article 10 of the Declaration of Rights of 1774, following the English guarantee of independence of the judiciary in 1689. Moreover, an appeal lay from the colonial courts to the Privy Council, which under the conditions of travel in those days was expensive, dilatory, and vexatious. In one case a colonial legislature voted to pay the expenses of a litigant, successful in the colonial court, who had to defend his judgment at Westminster. Colonial legislatures often sought to limit the time for appeals to the Privy Council, or to limit the cases in which they might be brought, or to require leave of the colonial court to bring them. Such statutes were frequently "disallowed." In any event the Privy Council did not hold itself bound by them and for what it considered good cause would extend the time or grant leave when the colonial court had refused it. The separation of powers, which became fundamental in our constitutional law, was urged already in colonial America as a relief from excessive concentration of political power.

Most significant of all, however, the foundation was laid for a real constitutional law: for a body of precepts enforced by the courts in the ordinary course of ordinary legal proceedings; for guarantees which those aggrieved could invoke in the courts as part of the law of the land which judges were bound to administer, not mere pious exhortations which legislatures and executives might obey or disregard as they liked. American lawyers of the colonial era were brought up on the idea of courts refusing to apply statutes in contravention of the fundamental law or law of the land.

Thus there are three points of origin of what has been called the American doctrine of the power of courts with respect to unconstitutional legislation: a power which it should be said in passing is not peculiar to America but has had to be asserted under written constitutions in Canada, in Australia, in South Africa, and in Eire. One is the idea of the law of the land as expounded in Coke's *Second Institute*. A second is Coke's doctrine that statutes contrary to common right and reason and so to fundamental law were void, or, as the medieval cases said, impertinent to be observed. The third is the practice, familiar to American lawyers of the colonial era, of appeals to the Privy Council in which statutes enacted by colonial legislatures were held void, i.e. not to be the basis of judicial decision, because in conflict with some provision of the colonial or provincial charter or in contravention of the common law, made by the charter the measure of lawmaking authority. That statutes could be scrutinized to look into the basis of their authority and if in conflict with fundamental law must be disregarded was as much a matter of course to the American lawyer of the era of the Revolution as the doctrine of the absolute binding force of an act of Parliament is to the English lawyer of today. American lawyers were taught to believe in a fundamental law which, after the Revolution, they found declared in written constitutions. After 1688 there was no fundamental law superior to Parliament. But the law of the land still restrained the action of the crown and of officials.

In 1761, James Otis in Paxton's Case, arguing against

the writs of assistance, relies on Bonham's Case, Day v. Savadge, and City of London v. Wood, quoted from Viner's *Abridgment* (1742–53), a twenty-three-volume digest of English case law from the Year Books and the reports, the proceeds of which endowed Blackstone's professorship at Oxford. As Gray (afterwards Justice of the Supreme Court of the United States) says in his note to Paxton's Case in Quincy's Reports, the doctrine laid down by Coke in Bonham's Case "was repeatedly asserted by Otis and was a favorite one in the colonies before the Revolution." In John Adams' *Diary* he tells us of a number of suits brought in 1762 for penalties under a statute of the province, and of the argument of Jeremy Gridley, then leader of the bar. The words of the *Diary* are: "Authorities from Hobart's and Coke's Reports were produced . . . that a man shall not be judge in his own cause, and that an act of Parliament against natural equity, as that a man shall be judge in his own case would be void." After the Long Parliament ordered the publication of the *Second Institute,* Coke's teachings became commonplaces in New England. As far back as 1688 we are told in the Lambert MS that "the men of Massachusetts did much quote Lord Coke." Later, Hutchinson, speaking against the Stamp Act in 1765, says: "The prevailing reason . . . is that the act of Parliament is against Magna Charta and the natural rights of Englishmen," and therefore, "according to Lord Coke, null and void." Likewise, in a letter of that year Hutchinson writes: "Our friends to liberty take advantage of a maxim they find in Lord Coke, that an act of Parliament against Magna Charta or the peculiar rights of Englishmen is void."

In 1765, the effect of the Stamp Act, which required the papers necessary in carrying on the work of the courts in Massachusetts to be stamped, was to close all the courts for want of the required stamped paper. As this had a paralyzing effect upon business, the citizens of Boston, in town meeting, addressed a memorial to the governor in council praying the governor to give directions to open the courts. John Adams and James Otis argued for the memorial. Adams' argument went on two propositions: (1.) that the statute was against common right and reason in that it imposed a tax without the consent of the people or their representatives, and (2.) that it contravened chapter 40 of Magna Carta by denying or delaying justice. Otis also argued from the guarantee against denying or delaying justice and cited Coke.

Perhaps the most striking example of general opinion of American lawyers in the colonies as to the power of courts with respect to statutes contrary to fundamental law is to be seen in the action of the County Court of Northampton County, Virginia, in 1766. The court was confronted with the same situation that had closed the courts in Boston. The Stamp Act required the use of stamped paper for legal proceedings and no stamped paper was at hand. If the act was followed the business of the courts must stop. The County Court in Virginia at that time was a superior court of record with jurisdiction of all cases at law and equity involving more than twenty shillings. It was held before the magistrates of the county and the decisions of a bench of seven were binding upon all the other county courts. Accordingly, a petition to open the court was presented and special justices were added to the regular bench of five. The court held that the Stamp Act did not "bind, affect, or concern the inhabitants of this colony," or, in other words, that it was impertinent to be observed, and that public business could go on without the officials incurring penalties under the act. Repeal of the statute prevented the matter going further, but the assurance with which the matter was determined shows how firmly the idea of judicial power in such cases was rooted in the mind of the profession.

If anything more had been needed to familiarize Americans with judicial scrutiny of the validity of legislation, review by the Privy Council of judgments of colonial courts based on colonial statutes sufficed. The charters of Massachusetts, Virginia, and Georgia allowed enactment of laws "not contrary to the laws of England." The charters of Rhode Island, Pennsylvania (1681), and Maryland permitted legislation "not repugnant to the laws of England." The Frame of Government of Pennsylvania (1683) provided that no laws should be enacted "repugnant to the charter." The charter of Delaware contained a short bill of rights taken from the Charter of Privileges of Pennsylvania (1701). The charter of Carolina, serving for both North and South Carolina, allowed enactment of "laws agreeable to the laws and customs of England." Thus in each of the colonies there was from the beginning a legal measure of the validity of legislation enforceable by appeal to the Privy Council. This power was exercised in some notable instances, as where colonial legislation providing for descent of land to all children equally, instead of to the eldest son as at common law, was held invalid and settlement of an estate in conformity to that legislation was set aside.

Thus the lawyers of America were well prepared for a written constitution and bill of rights such as was adopted in Virginia just before the Declaration of Independence.

4

From the Revolution to the Constitution

BEFORE THE DECLARATION OF INDEPENDENCE the Continental Congress had recommended to each colony to form independent state governments. Virginia was the first to do so by a written constitution. New Jersey, Pennsylvania, Delaware, Maryland, and North Carolina followed the same year. In 1776, Connecticut declared independence but went on under its charter till 1818. Before the close of the Revolutionary War, all the states except New Hampshire, Rhode Island, and Connecticut had adopted constitutions. In New Hampshire, the constitution first submitted failed of adoption, but a new draft was adopted in 1784. Rhode Island went on under its colonial charter as a constitution till 1842. The idea of a written constitution had the Instrument of Government under the Commonwealth for a precedent, but it was familiar to the lawyers of the Revolution both from the charters they had read of in their law books and from the charters under which the colonial and provincial governments had been operating, and to which they had been accustomed to refer the powers of magistrates and legislatures. The province was governed under a charter issued by the king. The state was to be governed by a charter promulgated by a sovereign people.

Six of these constitutions adopted before 1787 contained full bills of rights, of which that in Virginia was the first.

The other six put from one to four guarantees of particular rights in the text, just as the original federal Constitution contained no bill of rights but did include a certain number of provisions of that nature. The idea of a separate declaration of rights, prefixed or appended to a constitution as a part thereof, came to prevail throughout the land. Since the federal Constitution was amended in 1791 to include a bill of rights, every subsequent state constitution has contained one. The idea goes back to the Articles of the Barons and Magna Carta, the Petition of Right, the English Bill of Rights of 1688, and the Declaration of Rights of the Continental Congress.

Bills of rights in state constitutions, since the federal Bill of Rights, have generally followed that model. But there was not a little diversity of items in those which came first. No less than thirty-three items are to be found, seven of them, however, only in one, and five more only in two. Those which appear in less than half of the first bills of rights are not all of them of slight importance. Two of them found a place in the federal Bill of Rights and have appeared generally in state constitutions since, namely, that no one is to be twice in jeopardy for the same offense and that no one is to be held for an infamous crime except upon indictment or presentment of a grand jury. The principle of three more found a place in the original Constitution of the United States, namely, the provision in Massachusetts and Maryland that no one was to be declared guilty of treason or felony by the legislature (in the form of prohibiting to the states enactment of bills of attainder or of pains and penalties), the provision in New Hampshire and Pennsylvania that private property was not to be taken for public use without compensation (in the form of prohibiting such taking without consent), and guarantee in Pennsylvania of the right to emigrate to another state (taken care of in the federal Constitution by the clause as to privileges and immunities of citizens). Of the others to be found in less than half, New Hampshire and Massachusetts guaranted impartial judges while Maryland guaranteed the independence of judges. In the federal Constitution this appears in a provision that the salaries of judges shall not be diminished during their term. State constitutions have generally adopted this. It comes from the English Bill of Rights and was the subject of a characteristically vigorous statement by Mr. Justice McCardie some years ago when Parliament disregarded it. New Hampshire and Massachusetts, which had had experience of the particular abuse on the eve of the Revolution, prohibited quartering of soldiers in private houses in time of peace. This was an abuse practiced also by Charles I and James II, and was denounced by the Petition of Right and by the English Bill of Rights which also denied the king an army without the consent of Parliament. Quartering of soldiers is also forbidden by the federal Bill of Rights. Maryland and North Carolina, following the Second Institute, prohibited monopolies. South Carolina had claimed the common-law guarantees in 1712 and they were established in the first constitutions in New York and Delaware. New Hampshire required penalties to be in proportion to the offense, something with which the recent theories of penal treatment, adjusted to the offender rather than to the offense, do not entirely agree, but which was suggested by such things as the intolerably excessive fine and bond exacted of the Earl of Devonshire at the instance of James II. Georgia, in its first constitution, prohibited excessive fines.

Of the provisions to be found in more than half of the

first bills of rights, three are in all of them, namely, guarantee of jury trial, of freedom of the press, and that the accused be informed of the charge against him and be confronted with the witnesses against him. Jury trial was especially insisted on because when judges were appointed and removed by the royal governors in order to secure judgments which the governors desired, the jury, even when chosen by a sheriff who was an appointee and tool of the governor, was the only assurance of a fair trial open to an accused or a litigant. It was for this reason that wide extensions of admiralty jurisdiction, since courts of admiralty proceed without juries, were so strongly objected to. Freedom of the press had attracted attention at the time of the trial of Zenger and was much in the public eye because of contemporary political prosecutions in England. The procedure in criminal trials which had come down from the Middle Ages was excessively hard upon accused persons prosecuted at the instance of the crown, and under the Stuarts the chances of the most innocent were often slender when the king was bent on conviction. The English Bill of Rights stressed the fundamental safeguards of accused persons and they have been provided for in all American constitutions from the beginning.

Next to these, the first bills of rights provided for the separation of powers, required by specially strong and strict provisions in Massachusetts, but put as fundamental also in New Hampshire, Maryland, Virginia, and North Carolina, and made the basis of the constitutional frame of government elsewhere, though not included in the bills of rights. Experience of centralization of all the powers of government in the Privy Council and Board of Trade and Plantations at Westminster had convinced the lawyers of the era of the Revolution that there was here something more than a political philosophical theory. The unanimity with which the idea was put into practical effect on the morrow of the Declaration of Independence shows that much more was behind it than a fashion.

Security of life, liberty, and property stand next, guaranteed in the bills of rights in New Hampshire, Massachusetts, Pennsylvania, Maryland, Virginia, and North Carolina, and by provisions in the first constitutions in Connecticut, South Carolina, and Georgia. Georgia adds a provision as to habeas corpus. I put these here as one, as in the federal Bill of Rights, but they stand as two, one of life and liberty and one of property, in New Hampshire and Massachusetts and in the constitution of Connecticut, while only life and liberty appear in the Bill of Rights of Virginia.

Five of the first bills of rights require that the accused have witnesses on his behalf. That he could not as government prosecutions were sometimes conducted was a shameful abuse. This abuse was forbidden in New Hampshire, Massachusetts, Pennsylvania, Maryland, and Virginia, and in the constitution in New Jersey. We are witnessing a return to this abuse in the denial of process for witnesses by administrative agencies which have the power of subpoena for their own case but refuse or hamper attempt to secure witnesses or documents on behalf of those against whom they are proceeding.

General warrants were forbidden in the first bills of rights in New Hampshire, Massachusetts, Maryland, Virginia, and North Carolina. This guarantee was put also in the federal Bill of Rights.

Five states secured the accused against being compelled to give evidence against himself, another provision incorporated in the federal Bill of Rights and caused by experience of serious abuses. Nowhere, perhaps, does the difficulty of maintaining a just balance between the general security and the individual life make so much trouble for the administration of criminal justice as at this point. The pressure to get convictions which has made the third degree a well-understood incident of criminal investigation requires the maintenance and enforcement of this provision. It was contained in the first bills of rights in Massachusetts, Pennsylvania, Maryland, Virginia, and North Carolina.

Cruel and unusual punishments were forbidden by the first bills of rights in New Hampshire, Massachusetts, Maryland, Virginia, and North Carolina. The political and religious prosecutions in the seventeenth century in England had seen some horrible examples of the most cruel punishments, such as whippings at the tail of a cart from Newgate to Tyburn, a distance of two miles and one-half, and the memory of them was still green. This provision also was incorporated in the federal Bill of Rights. It may be said that we do not do such things now and hence such provisions in bills of rights are no longer needed. We do not do such things officially. But brutal treatment of suspected persons in time of crimes arousing public indignation, and the most cruel lynchings and whippings by white caps and night riders, have not been unknown in this country in recent times. If they could have the sanction of legality or be authorized officially, in times of great excitement they might revive.

In five states also exaction of excessive bail was forbidden in the original bills of rights. This was a serious abuse under James II and also under royal governors in the colonies. Indeed, it is a well-known phenomenon today when a certain type of publicity-cultivating magistrate attracts attention by fixing extravagant bail in case of some sensational crime. It was forbidden in the English Bill of Rights and the federal Bill of Rights. New Hampshire, Massachusetts, Maryland, Virginia, and North Carolina secured against it in the first bills of rights. In all common-law jurisdictions the remedy of habeas corpus is available to secure a reasonable bail whenever some magistrate fixes it unreasonably.

New Hampshire, Massachusetts, Maryland, Virginia, and North Carolina provided that laws were not to be suspended. These provisions were directed at executive suspensions on the model of royal dispensings under the Stuarts, carried to the extreme by James II. But in this country in our formative era after the Revolution the legislatures at times sought to exercise such a power, for instance, in one case suspending the statute of limitations for a particular party as to a particular claim against a particular person. The courts have refused to give effect to such statutes.

Four states, New Hampshire, Massachusetts, Maryland, and North Carolina, guaranteed against retrospective or ex post facto laws. These were forbidden to state legislation by the original federal Constitution as to ex post facto laws, and retrospective laws affecting property have been regarded as deprivations without due process of law. The same four provided also in the words of Magna Carta that justice was not to be sold, denied, or delayed; an excellent ideal but as to delay very hard to enforce by legal machinery. In one state recently, however, the highest court found it possible to remedy an intolerable condition of delay in one locality by exercise of one of its common-law powers.

New Hampshire, Pennsylvania, Maryland, and Virginia provided that the military was to be in "strict subordination to the civil power," New Hampshire adding "at all times." South Carolina put a similar provision in the constitution of 1778. New Hampshire, Massachusetts, Maryland, and North Carolina provided also against levies, taxes, or imposts except by authority of the legislature. These provisions grew out of bad practices of Stuart kings and royal governors and did not become general.

Three bills of rights, those of New Hampshire, Pennsylvania, and Maryland, guaranteed counsel to accused persons. This was denied in treason cases in England until after the Revolution of 1688. In the state bills of rights and in the federal Bill of Rights it is guaranteed for all criminal prosecutions. In recent years abuses in criminal investigation and in procuring pleas of guilty have made our highest court very insistent upon this right. New Hampshire, Massachusetts, and Maryland also provided for trials in the vicinage, generally regarded as included in the guarantee of jury trial, since a jury is a body of twelve good and lawful men of the vicinage. The federal Bill of Rights, however, provides for trial by a jury of the state or district wherein the crime was committed, which district must have been previously ascertained by law, thus preventing legislative setting up of arbitrary districts after the event in order to try particular accused persons away from the neighborhood.

Unreasonable searches and seizures were forbidden by New Hampshire, Massachusetts, and Pennsylvania. This provision was incorporated also in the federal Bill of Rights and has been general in state bills of rights since.

One of the most interesting of the guarantees in the

first bills of rights is the right to bear arms, secured to the king's Protestant subjects by the English Bill of Rights since James II had sought to hold down a Protestant majority by disarming them while allowing a hostile minority to bear arms. It was guaranteed in Massachusetts, Pennsylvania, and North Carolina, and is provided for also in the federal Bill of Rights. James Wilson, one of the signers of the Declaration of Independence and framers of the Constitution and one of the first Justices of the Supreme Court of the United States, in his lectures on law in Philadelphia in 1791 said: "A revolution principle certainly is, and certainly should be taught as, a principle of the Constitution of the United States and of every State in the Union." His editor, writing in 1900, tells us of a "natural right of revolution" and that a "minority may as justifiably rebel as a majority," and obviously if either majority or minority are not permitted to bear arms they are in no position to exercise this natural right. This idea has a long history. Chapter 61 of Magna Carta recognizes a right of revolution or rebellion and provides for an orderly exercise of it in case the promises in the Great Charter are not kept. If the Puritan Revolution did not proceed after legal forms, the Revolution of 1688 at least sought to, and the Declaration of Independence set forth a case under natural law. Such things as the disarming of Uitlanders by the South African Republic before the Boer War, while the burghers were well armed, reminds us that the problem involved is not an easy one. But a legal right of the citizen to wage war on the government is something that cannot be admitted, and the provision in the Bill of Rights stands among legal provisions and could be given legal effect by the courts if the purpose was one which could be entertained by them. The eighteenth-century jurist conceived that a moral right because it was moral was therefore legal. As there were cases in which rebellion was morally justified, therefore there must be cases in which it was legally justified. If so, fundamental law must secure to individuals the means of asserting the right. But bearing arms today is a very different thing from what it was in the days of the embattled farmers who withstood the British in 1775. In the urban industrial society of today a general right to bear efficient arms so as to be enabled to resist oppression by the government would mean that gangs could exercise an extra-legal rule which would defeat the whole Bill of Rights. In 1833, Judge Story in his *Commentaries on the Constitution* said: "The right of the citizen to keep and bear arms has justly been considered the palladium of the liberties of a republic, since it offers a strong moral check against the usurpation and arbitrary power of rulers, and will generally, even if these are successful in the first instance, enable the people to resist and triumph over them." He has in mind the situation of the English kings who till the eighteenth century had no standing army of consequence and so were restrained by an armed body of subjects. But he has to admit the inadequacy of militia even in his day to meet the military needs of a great government and gives the subject up. Here is the one provision of the Bill of Rights that seems to have been able to achieve nothing for us.

Along with bills of rights, the separation of powers— the putting of legislative, executive, and judicial functions in distinct departments by a fundamental law, binding each and requiring each to keep within its legal bounds—is specially characteristic of our first constitutions and of American constitutions ever since. Analytically the bills of rights are bills of liberties. They define circumstances and situations and occasions in which politically organized society will keep its hands off and permit free, spontaneous, individual activity; they guarantee that the agents and agencies of politically organized society will not do certain things and will not do certain other things otherwise than in certain ways. But those liberties are hardly less secured by the separation of powers, as anyone who studies the operation of administrative agencies in present-day America becomes acutely aware. During the seventeenth century the colonies were proprietary. The Lord Proprietor or the Proprietors were owners, and supreme legislative, executive, and judiciary. Thus Georgia was owned and governed by trustees and we have full records showing how the trustees governed. For example, a man who had been defeated in litigation in the Town Court at Savannah wrote a letter to the trustees complaining about the judgment. The records show that the secretary read the letter to the trustees and without anything more they directed that a letter be sent to the governor at Savannah to order the court to reverse the judgment. Throughout the seventeenth century the colonies were struggling to establish their own lawmaking bodies. After local legislatures were well established there was still a complete centralization of power at Westminster. Legislation was subject to a final veto by the Privy Council within five years and this power kept Pennsylvania without a system of courts for twenty-one years because the Pennsylvanians would not provide for a separate court of equity. Also, as has been said above, the ultimate control of administration was at Westminster through instructions to the governors, and the Privy Council was the ultimate court of appeal. Moreover, within the province the government was practically in the hands of the governor and council. Bad results followed this complete centralization as they had followed from centralization of power in the king in England. It is easy to assume that such things as happened in England when the king could control the judges and in colonial America when the royal governor could control them would not happen in the improved world in which we live. But only the other day the Stavisky scandal in France showed what may happen where the judiciary is under the control of the executive. Moreover, it was not a matter only of independence of the judiciary. The provincial legislatures had exercised undistributed powers with no limitation beyond disallowance of laws by the Privy Council, or, if some one had sufficient means to appeal, reversal of judgments by the Privy Council where based upon a statute. They granted continuances in particular cases, granted particular litigants in particular cases exemption from particular provisions of the statute of limitations, granted probate of particular wills rejected by the courts, directed details of administration of particular estates, foreclosed particular liens by legislative acts, and enacted title to land out of one party and into another by what amounted to a legislative ejectment. It is no wonder that our first constitutions insisted upon the separation of powers much more than upon the details of political organization. Often the latter were left much as they were or were committed to legislation. We must remember the experience that led up to this.

A proposition has been urged that the decisive reason for the separation of powers is specialization; that it is not "the practical security of civil liberty but the organic reason that every function will be better fulfilled if its organ is specially directed to this particular end than if quite different functions are assigned to the same organ." Hence, it is argued, efficiency being the end, if the separation of powers stands today in the way of efficiency, the reason for it has ceased to exist and it should be discarded. But too high a price may be paid for efficiency, and experience had made Englishmen of the seventeenth and Americans of the eighteenth century well aware of this. As Mr. Justice Brandeis put it, "the doctrine of the separation of powers was adopted by the convention of 1787 not to promote efficiency but to preclude the exercise of arbitrary power. The purpose was not to avoid friction, but, by means of the inevitable friction incident to the distribution of the governmental powers among three departments, to save the people from autocracy."

For the most part our difficulties with the doctrine in the present generation have arisen from nineteenth-century analytical attempts to maintain theoretical absolute lines. It was assumed that every power and every type and item of governmental action must of necessity be referrable once for all, exclusively and for every purpose, to some one of the three departments of government so that it could be exercised by no other. The sound legal political sense of John Marshall saw long ago that there were powers of doubtful classification: that there were powers which analytically and historically or from both standpoints might be assigned to either of two departments. In such cases he saw it was a proper legislative function to assign exercise of the power to an appropriate department. But the state courts went rigidly on an extreme analytical theory, and it was not till the second decade of the present century that Marshall's solution became established in the face of analytical attempts to put everything for all purposes and exclusively in one place. We were awakened to the impossibility of the rigid analytical theory by the exigencies of rate-making for public utilities. When the Intermountain Rate Cases decided that the Interstate Commerce Commission could be given power to fix rates, a power which might well be classified either as legislative or as executive, the occasion for most of the attack upon our constitutional regime had passed. The courts and the profession came to see that many things such as regulation of procedure, of legal education, and of admission to the bar, if analytically they might be held legislative in nature, were historically judicial, and that application of standards, if historically judicial, might analytically be held executive in nature. Hence legislative turning the former over to the courts and the latter to administrative agencies did not derogate from the constitutional separation of powers. But the older analytical logical idea long hampered administration and led to dissatisfaction with the constitutional regime, where it was enough to do away with the mistaken application.

As a result of dissatisfaction with the bad adjustment between adjudication and administration which existed, especially in the state courts, a generation ago, writers on political science have attacked severely what had been a cardinal tenet of our constitutional law. Teachers have been telling us that the separation of powers was only a fashion of eighteenth-century political thought, derived from a forecast made by Aristotle, for there was nothing of the sort in his time, and a mistaken interpretation of the British polity of his time by Montesquieu. We are told that it is outmoded and ought to give way to the exigencies of efficient administration. Recently this has spread to at least one of the courts which intimates that this fundamental principle of our constitutions should not be taken too seriously under the conditions of the time. Nothing could be more mistaken. When in the controversies which led to the Declaration of Independence hostility to things English led to finding a philosophical basis for the rights which lawyers had learned as the rights of Englishmen, natural rights were put as the ground of what the English had learned from experience. The separation of powers was no more derived from political philosophy than the rights secured by the Bill of Rights. It was taken up as the result of experience and reinforced by reference to Montesquieu. Whether put as common-law rights or as natural rights, the liberties claimed by generations of Englishmen and insisted on by the colonists as their birthright were seen to be incompatible with unlimited centralized power.

Another characteristic idea of our American constitutional polity is expressed in the clause of the Constitution, repeated in constitutions in the states, that it is the supreme law of the land. This idea, which goes back to the medieval teaching and decision as to the law of the land and due process of law, as developed by Coke, has made the Bill of Rights an effective instrument for its purpose. The idea of judicial application of constitutional provisions and of judicial refusal to give effect to legislation repugnant to the Constitution or to official action in excess of powers provided by the Constitution, goes back to refusal of the common-law courts to give effect to acts of Parliament "impertinent to be observed" because dealing with matters beyond the reach of temporal power; to the doctrine of seventeenth-century common-law courts as to acts contrary to common right and reason; to a provision in the Instrument of Government in 1653; and to colonial experience of reversal of judgments based on colonial statutes contrary to the common law. There is a perfect continuity between these cases and those decided after 1789 in the Supreme Court of the United States and in the state courts. This is abundantly shown by a line of decisions between the Declaration of Independence and the Constitution.

First in order of time is the case of Holmes v. Walton, decided in New Jersey in 1780. One of the rights most prized and most insisted upon by Americans was trial by jury. It was guaranteed in emphatic language by the constitution of New Jersey in 1776. But just as the king disliked juries where he was anxious to get results in disregard of liberties, the newly established states, when the legislature was eager to force compliance with an unpopular statute, showed a tendency to avoid jury trial or commit cases to small more easily managed juries. Holmes v. Walton arose under such a statute. Trade between New Jersey, occupied by the Continental Army, and New York City, occupied by the British, was objectionable from a military standpoint but was very profitable. It was prohibited by a New Jersey statute of 1778 which provided for seizure of goods brought in in contravention of the statute, and to insure speedy disposition allowed a hearing before a justice of the peace and a jury of six. Under the act defendant seized goods in the possession of the plaintiff, as being brought from within the enemy lines, and on trial to a justice of the peace and six jurors there was a judgment of condemnation. The plaintiff then brought a writ of certiorari in the Supreme Court setting up that judgment was contrary to the Constitution since a jury meant a common-law jury of twelve. The judgment was reversed and it was ordered that possession be restored to the plaintiff. In other words, the state court refused to apply the state statute because it was in conflict with the state constitution.

Next in order of time is Commonwealth v. Caton, decided in Virginia in 1782. Down to 1776 the governor's council was part of the Legislative Assembly. The constitution of 1776 provided for a Senate and a House of Delegates and that the Senate could concur in, reject, or amend measures passed by the House. It also provided that the governor should "with the advice of the Council of State, have the power of granting reprieves or pardons, except where the prosecution shall have been carried on by the House of Delegates [i.e. impeachment] *or the law shall otherwise particularly direct,* in which case no reprieve or pardon shall be granted but by resolve of the House of Delegates." Caton and others were convicted under a statute which provided that the governor should not have the power to pardon persons convicted of treason under the act, but might suspend execution under the act till the General Assembly should determine whether they were proper objects of mercy. The House of Delegates passed a resolve granting a pardon but the Senate refused to concur, and the attorney general moved for execution. Counsel for the defendants argued (1.) that the statute providing for pardon by the General Assembly was unconstitutional; and (2.) that under the constitution the pardoning power was in the House of Delegates in cases where the governor was not allowed to pardon. As to the first point the attorney general argued that the court was not authorized to hold the Act of Assembly void. On this point all of the eight judges but one agreed that they could refuse to follow an act of the legislature in conflict with the constitution. One judge did not consider it necessary to pass on that question. All agreed, however, that because of the words above italicized the statute did not contravene the constitution. On the second point it refused to adopt the construction argued for and held that the House of Delegates could not pardon in cases under the statute. Among the judges was George Wythe, one of the great judges in the judicial history of Virginia, who pronounced vigorously for judicial power as to unconstitutional legislation, and John Blair, afterwards one of the framers of the constitution of the United States and Justice of the Supreme Court of the United States, who agreed with him.

In 1785, the question came up in Connecticut in the Symesbury Case and the Superior Court held that the proprietors of Symesbury could not have their grant from the colony taken from them or curtailed "even by the General Assembly" without their consent. The Supreme Court of Connecticut used the same language. The statute was enacted before the Revolution. But the court considered it void under the charter as contrary to Magna Carta and so contrary to the common law.

A statute of Rhode Island after the Revolution made paper money issued by the state legal tender and provided a penalty for refusing to accept it in payment for goods offered for sale; the statute to be enforced summarily by a special court of at least three judges, without a jury, "according to the laws of the land" with no continuance, "protection, privilege, or injunction" or appeal. In Trevett v. Weeden (1786), on an information for refusing to accept paper bills of the state in payment for meat, the five judges unanimously refused to act under the statute. Counsel for the defendant cited Bacon's *Abridgment* for the proposition taken from Coke in Bonham's Case that if a statute is repugnant the common law will control it and hold it void. The colonial charter which then stood as the state constitution required that statutes should not be "repugnant to the laws of England." Hence two of the judges spoke out plainly that the statute was unconstitutional in providing for trial without a jury. A third relied on the repugnancy in the words of the statute, which called for trial without a jury according to the laws of the land. The other two judges agreed in refusing to act under the statute but gave no reason. But the only reasons that could be urged were those given by their colleagues. The judges were sent for by the legislature after the manner of the Stuart kings and examined as to the ground of their action, but after a bold and convincing statement by one of them and advice that the judges could not be impeached, since lawyers took the same view of their duty, the matter was dropped.

Another case (Bayard v. Singleton) was decided in North Carolina in 1787, the very year in which the constitutional convention sat. The action was brought to recover a house and lot which had been conveyed to the defendant by a commissioner of forfeited estates of those who had taken the British side in the Revolution. A statute of 1786 required the courts in all cases where it was shown on affidavit that the defendant held under a sale from the commissioner to dismiss the suit summarily on motion. This had the effect of making the commissioner's deed reciting a sale conclusive and cutting off all inquiry as to the validity of the proceedings behind it. The bill of rights in the state constitution required trial by jury. Thus the statute not only cut off all inquiry as to whether the plaintiff had been lawfully deprived of his property, but it cut him off from trial of the facts by a jury. The highest court of the state overruled the motion to dismiss, saying that no act which the legislature could pass could repeal or alter the constitution, and used the traditional phrase, "fundamental law of the land."

This line of cases may be closed with one decided in South Carolina in 1792: after the Constitution of the United States, but showing how the matter was understood at the time the Constitution was adopted. In 1712, the legislature undertook to "confirm" a disputed title to a large tract of land in one of the claimants, and the question was whether the statute barred the claim of the adverse party. The court said that the statute was against common right and Magna Carta and *ipso facto* void. The bill of rights in the state constitution (1776) guaranteed against deprivation of property otherwise than by the "law of the land." But in 1712 the colonial charter required legislation to accord with "the laws and customs of England."

It will have been noticed that in three of these six cases the legislature undertook to provide for summary disposition of certain cases without trial by jury. In two others it undertook to take property from one and give it to another summarily. In another the lower house, thinking of itself as the "representatives of the people," undertook to act without the concurrence of the Senate. In other words, the legislatures in the formative era of our political institutions were found doing the same things that the Stuart kings had been doing in England. If the bills of rights were to be anything but empty exhortations, it was necessary for the judges to give the words "law of the land" in the constitutions their traditional meaning and hold the legislative acts contrary to the constitution "impertinent to be observed."

For historical reasons the Constitution of the United States is both a political and a legal document. Under it, political questions are often legal and legal questions to some extent political. In this respect our polity retains a prime characteristic of the English constitution from which it was largely derived. In the English polity there was no special public law differentiated from the ordinary law. Questions of the power and authority of those who acted as the agents of government were and still are dealt with by the ordinary courts, in ordinary legal proceedings, on the principles of law applicable to every one. Hence the legal side and the political side of the Constitution are not wholly separable. But a happy balance between the specific and the general, between the redress of specific grievances and guarantee of specific rights after the manner of Magna Carta and the general declaration of fundamental liberties after the manner of the eighteenth-century publicists, keeps these two sides in equilibrium. Very likely we do not justify an institution merely by showing that it is the culmination for the time being of a long line of continuous historical developemnt. Yet intuition, on which today it is the fashion to rely rather than upon history and reason, is likely to be crude reason applied to partial and limited experience. Experience developed by reason and reason working on and tested by experience have made and shaped our legal institutions.

Three types of ideas entered into the Constitution. The political ideas are largely those of the Puritan Revolution. The legal ideas are those of the seventeenth-century contests between the English courts and the crown. The philosophical ideas are those of the eighteenth century which culminated in the French Declaration of the Rights of Man. There is a close kinship of these ideas. The political ideas are those of an era of revolt from authority: of individual interpretation of the Bible and nonconformity in religious organization, and of consociation rather than subordination in government. They are ideas of the primacy of the individual man as the moral and so the political unit. The legal ideas are those of the relationally organized society of medieval England, in which the king was a great landlord in relation with his tenants, involving reciprocal rights and duties, as defined in Magna Carta, but reshaped and restated by the courts and lawyers of the seventeenth century to the exigencies of a polity in which the king was governor rather than landlord. The idea of legal limits to the authority of those who wield governmental power, enforced as the law of the land in ordinary legal proceedings in the courts, had become basic in the English polity and was claimed by Americans as no less a heritage than their English speech. So, too, the idea that the acts of those who wield governmental power must be reasonable, not arbitrary and unreasonable, as a legal requirement given effect in the course of ordinary proceedings in the courts, had been taken to be the law of the land or due process of law, and was held firmly by the common-law lawyers and courts in the seventeenth century. We retained the two ideas as they came to us from Coke, confirmed by experience of centralized government at Westminster, the conduct of affairs by royal governors, and the arbitrariness of legislatures.

Turning to the development of the Constitution after its adoption, we have to notice that it contains three types of provisions. It prescribes the framework of government and prescribes limits of the lawful authority of the several organs and agencies of government. It guarantees certain rights to the individuals subject to the authority of government and defines and protects liberties, that is, areas of nonrestraint of men's natural faculties of action. Also it contains what are in effect exhortations as to how government ought to be carried on.

Of the provisions as to the framework of government, those which define authorities and spheres of action involve legal conceptions, legal principles, and sometimes rules of law. Both these and the primarily legal precepts which guarantee rights and secure liberties call for judicial interpretation and application. Thus even the political side of the Constitution requires constitutional law. There are laws in the text of the Constitution, but it is law that gives life to the laws and to the text. It is important to bear this in mind because interpretation and application are not the same thing and much misunderstanding of our constitutional law arises from confusing them. Laws call for interpretation and law determines how that interpretation shall proceed. As to many laws the main difficulty is interpretation, finding the limits and content of the rule, and when interpreted, application is a simple matter of logical fitting of facts to rule. As to many others, however, interpretation is a simple matter and the whole difficulty is in application, which is not and cannot be wholly logical but demands a certain moral or, in case of constitutional standards, a certain political judgment. It cannot be emphasized too strongly that even the strictly legal precepts of the Constitution are not all of one kind, and do not admit of precisely the same treatment by the courts. Thus the task of constitutional law is by no means an easy one which may be understood offhand even by the lawyer.

Of the legal precepts in the Constitution, some are rules,

making definite detailed provisions for definite detailed states of fact. Most of these are prohibitions either expressly or in effect guaranteeing certain liberties against impairment by government or safeguarding them by certain limitations of governmental power or certain prescribed modes of governmental interference. As soon as it was settled, under the leadership of Marshall, that a liberal interpretation of these grants of power, subject to the principles established by the Ninth and Tenth Amendments, was to prevail, interpretation ceased to give much trouble since most of the provisions had a well-recorded history which made their legal import fairly clear. But it should be borne in mind that the prescribings of limits and the guarantees would be nugatory if treated only as pious exhortations or appeals to the forbearance and good judgment of legislature or executive. This is shown amply, if it needed to be shown, by the fate of the declarations of the rights of man in Continental and Latin American constitutions.

Another type of legal precept establishes principles. That is, it lays down authoritative premises for legal reasoning rather than making definite detailed provisions for any definite detailed state of fact. Such principles are to be found, for example, in the Ninth and Tenth Amendments. They do not call for interpretation. But when the court is called on to interpret a rule, especially a rule defining the limits of state and national power or the limitations on governmental authority, they furnish authoritative starting points from which the court's reasoning may proceed.

Still another type of legal precept establishes legal conceptions, that is, authoritative categories to which questions may be referred with the result that certain rules, principles, and standards become applicable. Such are interstate commerce, full faith and credit, obligation of contract, privileges and immunities of citizens, equal protection of the laws. These categories are left undefined. They are not historically given nor are they common-law categories. They have required judicial ascertainment of their limits and their content. Indeed, judicial development of these categories could not have been avoided if they were to mean anything as preserving a balance between state and nation. To leave them to legislative and executive definition for each case of controversy for the time being would put this balance at the destructive mercy of politics, the very thing against which they were intended to guard.

In addition, some, and not the least important, of the legal precepts in the Constitution lay down standards to which governmental action is to be held to conform. An example is the standard of due process of law established by the Fifth and Fourteenth Amendments. History makes the interpretation clear enough. Governmental action is not to be arbitrary and unreasonable. But the reasonable is not defined by any rule or principle of law. Due process of law is a standard to be applied according to the ever-changing circumstances of time and place, like the legal standard of due care, or of fair conduct of a fiduciary, or of reasonable service and reasonable facilities of a public utility in private law. It involves all the difficulties involved in application of the latter standards and indeed more, because it calls for a measure of political judgment also. It is here that most of the complaints as to our Constitution and our constitutional law have arisen and it is here, too, that they have had their chief justification. In the last third of the nineteenth century reasonableness was looked at in the abstract rather than concretely. The change from demanding abstract reasonableness to looking to concrete reasonableness in 1916 was a significant advance in our constitutional law and was in the spirit of the common law.

A few provisions in the original Constitution were in the nature of a bill of rights. One of them, namely, the provision against suspension of the writ of habeas corpus, goes back to Coke's commentary on Magna Carta. Another, the prohibition of bills of attainder and bills of pains and penalties, grew out of experience of what have been aptly called legislative lynchings during and after the Revolution. In the excitement of the time statutes convicting of crime and imposing punishment of death (bills of attainder) or of imprisonment or forfeiture of property (bills of pains and penalties) were enacted capriciously and were procured on grounds of ill will in relatively trivial cases as well as in the grave cases involving danger to the Commonwealth for which they were supposed to be reserved. The historian of these acts tells us that "the passion and prejudice of the populace failed, at times, to distinguish between mere political sentiment and giving aid and comfort to the enemy." Tucker, writing in 1803, when the memory of such acts was fresh, said that an act of attainder was "a legislative declaration of the guilt of a party without trial, without a hearing, and often without the examination of witnesses."

No bill of rights was included in the original Constitution. But people were justly fearful that the new strong central government they were setting up would do the things or some of the things they had endured from centralized government at Westminster and from central governments in the provinces. Hence the Constitution was only ratified on assurance that a bill of rights should at once be added. In comparison with the earlier state bills of rights, the first nine amendments are more concise and compact. They deal with the more vital points, with less detail than many of the state constitutions, but leave out nothing of real importance. One provision, however, not contained in the first state constitutions, is an everyday safeguard of property, namely, the provision that private property is not to be taken for public use without just compensation. This has been included in the state bills of rights ever since. It runs back to Magna Carta. In the Articles of the Barons they asked that the constable or other bailiff (i.e. agent) of the king should not take grain or other chattels without paying cash down therefor, nor the sheriff or bailiff of the king take horses or carts of any free man for carriage on the king's account, without the owner's consent, nor the king or his bailiff take another's wood for his castle or other affairs without consent, and it was so provided in chapters 29, 30, and 31 of Magna Carta. In the reissue of the Great Charter later it is provided that no sheriff or bailiff of the king shall take the horses or carts of any man to make carriage unless he pays the customary price. Fortescue tells how in fifteenth-century France private property was continually taken for the king's soldiers with no compensation, whereas in England of that time the king could only take necessaries for his household at a reasonable price. Apparently the Stuarts sought only to compel forced loans of money and impose taxes and levies under claim of prerogative, but not to take property in specie. So Coke's commentary on the relevant chapters of Magna Carta is very brief. But the principle behind the specific provisions was clear, and experience of impressments of property during the Revolution led to putting the principle in the federal Bill of Rights.

Nowadays, in a time of the cult of absolutism, reliance on force rather than reason, and of current philosophies which disparage liberty and rate satisfaction of material wants as the highest good and the end of government, those who write on the science of government are prone to speak lightly of these constitutional provisions. To some they are inconsistent with democracy. It is assumed that democracy must be an absolute rule of a majority for the time being, and the idea of limitations on those who exercise the powers of a politically organized society under a democracy is rejected. In the same way, under the Tudors and Stuarts many thought that monarchy must be the absolute rule of an autocratic king and that limitations on what his agents could do were obsolescent remnants from the feudal regime. But, as Mr. Justice Miller put it, the spirit of our government is opposed to the deposit of unlimited power anywhere. Democracy does not require that its agents have absolute power and be, like the Eastern Roman emperor, free from the laws. A generation which is willing to give up the legal inheritance of Americans and set up a regime of absolute rule of a majority may find that in the event it is under the absolute rule of a leader of the majority.

Other ideas urged recently are that to those who drafted the constitutional provisions liberty meant only freedom from imprisonment and due process of law meant only procedural regularity. But the terms "liberty" and "due process" were legal terms with well-understood meanings known to lawyers; and when one notes the names of the great lawyers who signed the original Constitution—

one future Chief Justice and two future Justices of the Supreme Court of the United States, a Chief Justice of New Jersey, and many who were then accounted leaders of the profession, it is idle to assume that they did not know the significance of the words they used.

Again, we hear many urge today that judicial power as to unconstitutional legislation is something never intended and its exercise is a judicial usurpation. But the clear understanding of American lawyers before the Revolution, based on the seventeenth-century books in which they had been taught, the unanimous course of decision after independence and down to the adoption of the Constitution, not to speak of the writings of two of the prime movers in the convention which drafted the instrument, are abundant proof to the contrary. Moreover, to those lawyers the result was involved in the pronouncement that the Constitution was the supreme law of the land. Again, a written constitution, according to the ideas of the English-speaking world, means a body of law enforceable as such. The Judicial Committee of the Privy Council had to come to this as to the constitution of Canada. The courts of Canada, Australia, and Eire find themselves called on to decide constitutional questions, and the highest court of the South African Republic held a legislative act contrary to the *grondwet* or fundamental law invalid upon reasoning derived from the authorities of the Civil Law. A tyrannical executive removed the court in the latter case. But the oppressions which the decision of the court held unlawful brought on the Boer War, the disappearance of the South African Republic, and a written constitution for the Dominion of South Africa.

Our constitutional government, founded in the experience of English-speaking peoples, has survived tran-

sition from thirteen states along the Atlantic to a continental empire, survived the struggle between a society of
planters and one of traders and manufacturers, survived
civil war and come out stronger, survived entry into
world affairs, survived transition from a homogeneous
folk of one stock to a melting pot of races and peoples.
Not only has it survived, it has made a land to which
people from every part of the world have sought and seek
to come to enjoy liberty and opportunity under law. Unless the nature of man has greatly changed, there is no
good reason why it should not survive the struggles incident to modern industrial development and economic
unification.

English constitutional monarchy, based on the idea of
legal limitation of governmental action, legal responsibility of officials, and judicial securing of the rights of individuals against arbitrary action, survived from the
Middle Ages, through the sixteenth- and seventeenth-
century era of centralization and the eighteenth-century
era of absolute governments, into the nineteenth century,
and in the twentieth century its latest form of a constitutional administrative regime has grown strong while
much of the world was turning to dictators and administrative absolutism. Our constitutional democracy may
survive this era of centralization and economic unification
for like reasons. Whether rule is borne by Rex or by Demos,
a ruler ruling reasonably under God and the law founds
his kingdom on a rock.

Source Materials Illustrating the Text

Charter of Liberties, Henry I, 1100 (secs. 2, 3, 4, 7, 8. Translated from Stubbs, *Select Charters and Other Illustrations of English Constitutional History*).

2. If any of my barons, counts, or others who hold of me shall have died his heir shall not redeem his land as he did in the time of my brother but shall relieve it by a just and legal relief. Likewise also the tenants of my barons shall relieve their lands from their landlords by a just and legal relief.

3. And if any of my barons or other of my tenants has wished to give in marriage his daughter or sister or granddaughter or kinswoman, thereupon let him speak with me; but neither will I take anything of his for this license nor will I forbid his giving her except if he wishes to join her to my enemy. And if an heiress daughter of a deceased baron or tenant of mine has remained I will give her with her land by the advice of my barons. And if a wife of a deceased husband has remained and has been without children, she shall have her dower and marriage [1] and I will not give her to a husband unless according to her will.

4. But if a wife shall remain with children, she shall have her dower and marriage so long as she has held her body lawfully and I will not give her unless according to her will. And either the wife or another of the relatives who most justly ought to be shall be guardian of the lands and of the children. And I command that my barons likewise hold themselves in check towards the sons and daughters and wives of their tenants.

7. And if any of my barons or tenants is enfeebled, according as he himself shall give or shall arrange to give his money, so I concede it to be given. But if he, prevented either by arms or by infirmity, shall not have given or arranged to give his money, let his wife or children or parents or his lawful men [2] divide it for his soul as shall seem best to them.

1. I.e. a sum of money exacted as the value of marriage of one under the guardianship of the landlord.
2. I.e. men owing him allegiance.

8. If any one of my barons or tenants has transgressed the law he shall not give security in amercement of his money as he did in the time of my father or of my brother, but he shall make amends according to the measure of the transgression, as amends were made before the time of my father in the time of my other predecessors. But if he has been convicted of treachery or crime he shall make amends as may be just.

Assize of Clarendon, 1166.

1. First the said King Henry by the advice of all his barons, for preserving the peace and maintaining justice, has enacted by the advice of all his barons that inquiry be made in each county, and in each hundred, by twelve more lawful men of the hundred and four more lawful men of every vill upon oath that they speak the truth: whether in their hundred or vill there is any man who is accused or known to be robber or murderer or thief or any who has been receiver of robbers or murderers or thieves after the lord King became King.[3] And let the justices inquire of this before themselves and the sheriff before himself.

Glanvill, *de legibus et consuetudinibus regni Angliae*, 1187–89.[4]

Bk. I, chap. 5. When anyone complains to the lord King concerning his fee or freehold, if the complaint is such that it ought or that the lord King wishes it to be decided in his court, then he who complains shall have such a writ of summons:

Chap. 6. The King to the Sheriff, Greeting. Command A that without delay he render to B one hide of land in such a vill of which the said B complains that the aforesaid A deforces him; and unless he does so summon him by good summoners that he be there before me or my justices on the day after the end of the octave of Easter to show why he did not do it. And have there the summoners and this writ.

Bk. II, chap. 7. Moreover that assize [i.e. the grand assize] is a certain royal benefit bestowed upon the people by the clemency of the prince with the advice of the lords, by which the integrity of the life and civil condition of men is so wholesomely cared for that,

3. This is the origin of the grand jury.
4. *On the Laws and Customs of the Kingdom of England.*

retaining what any one possesses of land in freehold, men may decline the doubtful event of trial by battle. . . .

Chap. 10. By such writs [described in chaps. 8 and 9] the tenant [5] seeks peace and puts himself on the assize until his adversary coming to court seeks another writ that by four lawful knights of the county and of the vicinage there be chosen twelve lawful knights of the same vicinage who shall say on their oath which of the litigants has the greater right in the land sought. . . .[6]

Chap. 12. . . . But it should be noted that where four knights, prepared to choose the others, appear in court on the day fixed for them, a certain just and equitable constitution [7] has been enacted according to which on advice the case is wont to be so expedited that whether or not the tenant appears nevertheless choice [of the twelve] is made by the four knights upon their oath. . . .

Chap. 14. But choice having been made of the twelve knights they are to be summoned to come to court prepared to say upon their oath which of them—the tenant or the demandant—has the greater right in his demand. . . .

Chap. 17. When the assize proceeds to making the recognition itself, either the right will be well known to the jurors themselves or some will know and others will not know or all will be ignorant. If none of them know the truth of the matter and they have testified to this upon their oath, it will be necessary to have recourse to others until such are found as know the truth of the matter. But if some know the truth of the matter and some do not, those who do not being rejected, others are to be called to court until twelve at least are found in agreement. Likewise if some say for one and some for the other of the litigants, others are to be added until twelve at least have agreed on one side or the other. Moreover each of those who are called for this purpose ought to swear that they will not say what is false nor conceal the truth and this is to be held as to the knowledge of those who swear in this matter: there is exacted knowledge which they have from their own seeing and hearing and from the words of their fathers and of others in whom they have faith as of their own.

5. I.e. the one in possession—the defendant.
6. This is the trial jury.
7. Latin *constitutio*, an enactment of the Roman emperor.

Articles of the Barons, 1215 (translated from Stubbs, *Select Charters and Other Illustrations of English Constitutional History*).

These are the articles which the Barons ask and the lord King concedes.

1. After the death of their ancestors heirs of full age shall have their inheritance by the old relief, to be expressed in the charter.

2. Heirs who are under age and have been in guardianship, when they come of age shall have their inheritance without relief and fine.

3. The guardian of the land of an heir shall take reasonable issues, customs, and services, without destruction and waste of his men and property; and the guardian shall maintain from the issues of that land the houses, enclosures, warrens, ponds, and mills belonging to the land; and that the heirs shall be so married as not to be disparaged and by the advice of their near relatives.

4. Let a widow give nothing for her dower or marriage after the death of her husband, but let her remain in her house forty days after his death, and within that term let dower be assigned her; and let her have at once her marriage and inheritance.

5. The king or bailiff shall not seize any land for debt while the chattels of the debtor are sufficient; nor shall the sureties of the debtor be distrained when the principal debtor suffices for payment; but if the principal debtor has defaulted in payment, if the sureties will, let them have the lands of the debtor until he shall have fully paid the debt unless the principal debtor can show he is fully quit thereof against the sureties.

6. The king shall not concede to any baron that he may take aid [8] from his free men except for redeeming his body, and making his eldest son a knight, and marrying his oldest daughter; and he shall do this by a reasonable aid.

7. Let no one do more service for a knight's fee than is due from it.

8. That common pleas shall not follow the court of the lord king but shall be assigned in some certain place; and that recognitions [9]

---

8. A benevolence granted by a tenant to his lord in time of distress, which became a regular incident of tenure, demandable of right.

9. See the extracts from Glanvill, supra.

be taken in the same counties in this manner: That the king and two justices four times a year, who with four knights of the same county, chosen by the county, take assises of novel disseisin, death of ancestor, and last presentation, and no one shall be summoned on this account but the jurors and the two parties.

9. That a free man shall be amerced for a small offense according to the measure of the offense, and for a great offense according to the magnitude of the offense, saving his condition, and a villein in the same manner, saving his implements of husbandry, and a merchant in the same way, saving his merchandise, by the oath of honest men of the vicinage.

15. If any tenant of the king dies, it shall be allowable for the sheriff or other bailiff of the king to seize and inventory his chattels by the view of lawful men, so, nevertheless that nothing of them is removed until it is fully known whether he owes some liquidated debt to the lord king; and when the debt of the king is paid the residue shall be relinquished to the executors for carrying out the testament of the deceased; and if nothing is owing to the king let all chattels come to the deceased.

18. Let not the constable or other bailiff take grain or other chattels unless immediately he pays cash therefor except if he can have credit by the will of the seller.

19. Let not the constable be able to distrain any knight to pay money for castle guard if he wishes to do guard in person or by other honest man if for reasonable cause he cannot do it himself; and if the king has taken him in the army let him be quit of the guard according to the length of time.

20. Let not the sheriff or the bailiff of the king or anyone else take horses or carts of any free man for making carriage unless with his consent.

21. Let not the king or his bailiff take another's wood for his castle or other his affairs unless by the consent of the one whose wood it is.

25. If any one is disseised or delayed by the king of lands, liberties, or his right, without a judgment, let him be restored immediately, and if a contention has arisen about this, then let it be disposed of by the judgment of twenty-five barons; and let those who have been disseised by the father or brother of the king have right without delay by the judgment of their peers in the court of the king . . .

26. Let nothing be paid for a writ of inquiry of life or limb, but let it be granted freely without price and not denied.

28. Let no bailiff be able to put any one to his law [1] by his own simple word without credible witnesses.

29. Let not the body of a free man be taken; let him not be imprisoned nor disseised nor outlawed nor exiled nor destroyed in any way, nor let the king send upon him forcibly unless by the judgment of his peers or by the laws of the land.

30. Let not right and law be sold or delayed or forbidden.

31. That merchants have safe conduct to go and come for buying and selling without any unjust forcible exactions, according to the old and right customs.

32. Let no scutage or aid be imposed in the kingdom unless by the common counsel of the kingdom unless for ransoming the body of the king and making his eldest son a knight and once marrying the oldest daughter; and for this let there be a reasonable aid. Let it be in like manner as to exactions and aids from the city of London and other cities which have liberties therefrom and that the city of London have fully its old liberties and free customs both by water and by land.

33. That everyone be allowed to go from the kingdom and return, saving faith to the lord king, unless in time of war for some short time for the common utility of the kingdom.

Magna Carta, 1215 (McKechnie's Translation).

1. In the first place we have granted to God, and by this our present charter confirmed for us and our heirs for ever that the English church shall be free, and shall have her rights entire, and her liberties inviolate; and we will that it be thus observed; which is apparent from this that the freedom of elections, which is reckoned most important and very essential to the English church, we, of our pure and unconstrained will, did grant, and did by our charter confirm and did obtain the ratification of the same from our lord, Pope Innocent III., before the quarrel arose between us and our barons, and this we will observe, and our will is that it be observed in good faith by our heirs for ever. We have also granted to all free men of our kingdom, for us and our heirs for ever, all the

1. I.e. compel him to acquit himself by compurgation.

underwritten liberties, to be had and held by them and their heirs, of us and our heirs for ever.

2. If any of our earls or barons, or others, holding of us in chief by military service shall have died, and at the time of his death his heir shall be of full age and owe "relief," he shall have his inheritance on payment of the ancient relief, namely the heir or heirs of an earl, £100 for a whole earl's barony; the heir or heirs of a baron, £100 for a whole barony; the heir or heirs of a knight, 100s. at most for a whole knight's fee; and whoever owes less let him give less, according to the ancient custom of fiefs.

3. If, however, the heir of any one of the aforesaid has been under age and in wardship, let him have his inheritance without relief and without fine when he comes of age.

4. The guardian of the land of an heir who is thus under age, shall take from the land of the heir nothing but reasonable produce, reasonable customs, and reasonable services, and that without destruction or waste of men or goods; and if we have committed the wardship of the lands of any such minor to the sheriff, or to any other who is responsible to us for its issues, and he has made destruction or waste of what he holds in wardship, we will take of him amends, and the land shall be committed to two lawful and discreet men of that fee, who shall be responsible to us for the issues, or to him to whom we shall assign them; and if we have given or sold the wardship of any such land to someone and he has therein made destruction or waste, he shall lose that wardship, and it shall be transferred to two lawful and discreet men of that fief, who shall be responsible to us in like manner as aforesaid.

5. The guardian, morever, so long as he has the wardship of the land, shall keep up the houses, parks, places for livestock, fishponds, mills, and other things pertaining to the land, out of the issues of the same land; and he shall restore to the heir, when he has come to full age, all his land, stocked with ploughs and implements of husbandry, according as the season of husbandry shall require, and the issues of the land can reasonably bear.

6. Heirs shall be married without disparagement, yet so that before the marriage takes place the nearest in blood to that heir shall have notice.

7. A widow, after the death of her husband, shall forwith and without difficulty have her marriage portion and inheritance; nor

shall she give anything for her dower, or for her marriage portion, or for the inheritance which her husband and she held on the day of the death of that husband; and she may remain in the house of her husband for forty days after his death, within which time her dower shall be assigned to her.

8. Let no widow be compelled to marry, so long as she prefers to live without a husband; provided always that she gives security not to marry without our consent, if she holds of us, or without the consent of the lord of whom she holds, if she holds of another.

9. Neither we nor our bailiffs shall seize any land or rent for any debt, so long as the chattels of the debtor are sufficient to repay the debt; nor shall the sureties of the debtor be distrained so long as the principal debtor is able to satisfy the debt; and if the principal debtor shall fail to pay the debt, having nothing wherewith to pay it, then the sureties shall answer for the debt; and let them have the lands and rents of the debtor, if they desire them, until they are indemnified for the debt which they have paid for him, unless the principal debtor can show proof that he is discharged thereof as against the said sureties.

10. If one who has borrowed from the Jews any sum, great or small, die before that loan be repaid, the debt shall not bear interest while the heir is under age, of whomsoever he may hold; and if the debt fall into our hands, we will not take anything except the principal sum contained in the bond.

11. And if anyone die indebted to the Jews, his wife shall have her dower and pay nothing of that debt; and if any children of the deceased are left under age, necessaries shall be provided for them in keeping with the holding of the deceased; and out of the residue the debt shall be paid, reserving, however, service due to feudal lords; in like manner let it be done touching debts due to others than Jews.

12. No scutage nor aid shall be imposed in our kingdom, unless by common counsel of our kingdom, except for ransoming our person, for making our eldest son a knight, and for once marrying our eldest daughter; and for these there shall not be levied more than a reasonable aid. In like manner it shall be done concerning aids from the citizens of London.

13. And the citizens of London shall have all their ancient liberties and free customs, as well by land as by water; furthermore,

we decree and grant that all other cities, boroughs, towns, and ports shall have all their liberties and free customs.

14. And for obtaining the common counsel of the kingdom anent the assessing of an aid (except in the three cases aforesaid) or of a scutage, we will cause to be summoned the archbishops, bishops, abbots, earls, and greater barons, by our letters under seal; and we will moreover cause to be summoned generally, through our sheriff and bailiffs, all others who hold of us in chief, for a fixed date, namely, after the expiry of at least forty days, and at a fixed place; and in all letters of such summons we will specify the reason of the summons. And when the summons has thus been made, the business shall proceed on the day appointed, according to the counsel of such as are present, although not all who were summoned have come.

15. We will not for the future grant to anyone license to take an aid from his own free tenants, except to ransom his body, to make his eldest son a knight, and once to marry his eldest daughter; and on each of these occasions there shall be levied only a reasonable aid.

16. No one shall be compelled to perform greater service for a knight's fee, or for any other free tenement, than is due therefrom.

17. Common pleas shall not follow our court, but shall be held in some fixed place.

18. Inquests of *novel disseisin*,[2] of *mort d'ancestor*,[3] and of *darrein presentment*,[4] shall not be held elsewhere than in their own county courts, and that in manner following,—We, or, if we should be out of the realm, our chief justiciar, will send two justiciars through every county four times a year, who shall, along with four knights of the county chosen by the county, hold the said assizes in the county court, on the day and in the place of meeting of that court.

19. And if any of the said assizes cannot be taken on the day of the county court, let there remain of the knights and freeholders who were present at the county court on that day, as many as may

2. A real action to recover land of which the demandant has been recently disseised.

3. To recover land of which one was disseised where heir is the demandant.

4. To determine who was patron of a living.

be required for the efficient making of judgments, according as the business be more or less.

20. A freeman shall not be amerced for a small offense, except in accordance with the degree of the offense; and for a grave offense he shall be amerced in accordance with the gravity of his offense, yet saving always his "contenement"; and a merchant in the same way, saving his wares; and a villein shall be amerced in the same way, saving his wainage—if they have fallen into our mercy: and none of the aforesaid amercements shall be imposed except by the oath of honest men of the neighbourhood.

21. Earls and barons shall not be amerced except through their peers, and only in accordance with the degree of the offense.

22. A clerk shall not be amerced in respect of his lay holding except after the manner of the others aforesaid; further, he shall not be amerced in accordance with the extent of his church benefice.

23. No community or individual shall be compelled to make bridges at river-banks, except those who from of old were legally bound to do so.

24. No sheriff, constable, coroners, or others of our bailiffs, shall hold pleas of our Crown.

25. All counties, hundreds, wapentakes, and trithings (except our demesne manors) shall remain at the old rents, and without any additional payment.

26. If anyone holding of us a lay fief shall die, and our sheriff or bailiff shall exhibit our letters patent of summons for a debt which the deceased owed to us, it shall be lawful for our sheriff or bailiff to attach and catalogue chattels of the deceased, found upon the lay fief, to the value of that debt, at the sight of lawful men, provided always that nothing whatever be thence removed until the debt which is evident shall be fully paid to us; and the residue shall be left to the executors to fulfil the will of the deceased; and if there be nothing due from him to us, all the chattels shall go to the deceased, saving to his wife and children their reasonable shares.

27. If any freeman shall die intestate, his chattels shall be distributed by the hands of his nearest kinsfolk and friends, and under the supervision of the church, saving to everyone the debts which the deceased owed to him.

28. No constable or other bailiff of ours shall take corn or other provisions from anyone without immediately tendering money

therefor, unless he can have postponement thereof by permission of the seller.

29. No constable shall compel any knight to give money in lieu of castle-guard, when he is willing to perform it in his own person, or (if he himself cannot do it from any reasonable cause) then by another responsible man. Further, if we have led or sent him upon military service, he shall be relieved from guard in proportion to the time during which he has been on service because of us.

30. No sheriff or bailiff of ours, or any other person, shall take the horses or carts of any freeman for transport duty, against the will of the said freeman.

31. Neither we nor our bailiffs shall take, for our castles or for any other work of ours, wood which is not ours, against the will of the owner of that wood.

32. We will not retain beyond one year and one day, the lands of those who have been convicted of felony, and the lands shall thereafter be handed over to the lords of the fiefs.

33. All kydells for the future shall be removed altogether from Thames and Medway, and throughout all England, except upon the sea coast.

34. The writ which is called *praecipe* [5] shall not for the future be issued to anyone, concerning any tenement whereby a freeman may lose his court.[6]

35. Let 'there be one measure of wine throughout our whole realm; and one measure of ale; and one measure of corn, to wit, "the London quarter"; and one width of cloth (whether dyed, or russet, or halberget), to wit, two ells within the selvedges; of weights also let it be as of measures.

36. Nothing in future shall be given or taken for a writ of inquisition of life or limbs, but freely it shall be granted, and never denied.

37. If anyone holds of us by fee-farm, by socage, or by burgage, and holds also land of another lord by knight's service, we will not (by reason of that fee-farm, socage, or burgage) have the wardship of the heir, or of such land of his as is of the fief of that other;

5. "Command." A writ ordering a person to do some act or show cause why he should not do it.
6. I.e. his right to have the case heard in the court of the lord of whom he held.

nor shall we have wardship of that fee-farm, socage, or burgage, unless such fee-farm owes knight's service. We will not by reason of any petty serjeanty which anyone may hold of us by the service of rendering to us knives, arrows, or the like, have wardship of his heir or of the land which he holds of another lord by knight's service.

38. No bailiff for the future shall put any man to his "law" upon his own mere word of mouth, without credible witnesses brought for this purpose.

39. No freeman shall be arrested, or detained in prison, or deprived of his freehold, or outlawed, or banished, or in any way molested; and we will not set forth against him, nor send against him, unless by the lawful judgment of his peers and by the law of the land.

40. To no one will we sell, to no one will we refuse or delay, right or justice.

41. All merchants shall have safe and secure exit from England, and entry to England, with the right to tarry there and to move about as well by land as by water, for buying and selling by the ancient and right customs, quit from all evil tolls, except (in time of war) such merchants as are of the land at war with us. And if such are found in our land at the beginning of the war, they shall be detained, without injury to their bodies or goods, until information be received by us, or by our chief justiciar, how the merchants of our land found in the land at war with us are treated; and if our men are safe there, the others shall be safe in our land.

42. It shall be lawful in future for anyone (excepting always those imprisoned or outlawed in accordance with the law of the kingdom, and natives of any country at war with us, and merchants, who shall be treated as is above provided) to leave our kingdom and to return, safe and secure by land and water, except for a short period in time of war, on grounds of public policy—reserving always the allegiance due to us.

43. If one who holds of some escheat (such as the honour of Wallingford, of Nottingham, of Boulogne, or Lancaster, or of other escheats which are in our hands and are baronies) shall die, his heir shall give no other relief, and perform no other service to us than he would have done to the baron, if that barony had been in the baron's hand; and we shall hold it in the same manner in which the baron held it.

44. Men who dwell without the forest need not henceforth come before our justiciars of the forest upon a general summons, except those who are impleaded, or who have become sureties for any person or persons attached for forest offences.

45. We will appoint as justices, constables, sheriffs, or bailiffs only such as know the law of the realm and mean to observe it well.

46. All barons who have founded abbeys, concerning which they hold charters from the kings of England, or of which they have long-continued possession, shall have the wardship of them, when vacant, as they ought to have.

47. All forests that have been made such in our time shall forthwith be disafforested; and a similar course shall be followed with regard to river-banks that have been placed "in defence" by us in our time.

48. All evil customs connected with forests and warrens, foresters and warreners, sheriffs and their officers, river-banks and their wardens, shall immediately be inquired into in each county by twelve sworn knights of the same county chosen by the honest men of the same county, and shall, within forty days of the said inquest, be utterly abolished, so as never to be restored, provided always that we previously have intimation thereof, or our justiciar, if we should not be in England.

49. We will immediately restore all hostages and charters delivered to us by Englishmen, as sureties of the peace or of faithful service.

50. We will entirely remove from their bailiwicks, the relations of Gerard de Athyes (so that in future they shall have no bailiwick in England), namely Engelard de Cygony, Peter, Gyon, and Andrew of the Chancery, Gyon de Cygony, Geoffrey de Martyn with his brothers, Philip Mark with his brothers and his nephew Geoffrey, and the whole brood of the same.

51. As soon as peace is restored, we will banish from the Kingdom all foreignborn knights, cross-bowmen, serjeants, and mercenary soldiers, who have come with horses and arms to the kingdom's hurt.

52. If anyone has been dispossessed or removed by us, without the legal judgment of his peers, from his lands, castles, franchises, or from his right, we will immediately restore them to him; and if a dispute arise over this, then let it be decided by the five-and-twenty barons of whom mention is made below in the clause for

securing the peace. Moreover, for all those possessions, from which any one has, without the lawful judgment of his peers, been disseised or removed, by our father, King Henry, or by our brother, King Richard, and which we retain in our hand (or which are possessed by others, to whom we are bound to warrant them) we shall have respite until the usual term of crusaders; excepting those things about which a plea has been raised, or an inquest made by our order, before our taking of the cross; but as soon as we return from our expedition (or if perchance we desist from the expedition) we will immediately grant full justice therein.

53. We shall have, moreover, the same respite and in the same manner in rendering justice concerning the disafforestation or retention of those forests which Henry our father and Richard our brother afforested, and concerning the wardship of lands which are of the fief of another (namely, such wardships as we have hitherto had by reason of a fief which anyone held of us by knight's service), and concerning abbeys found on other fiefs than our own, in which the lord of the fee claims to have right; and when we have returned, or if we desist from our expedition, we will imemdiately grant full justice to all who complain of such things.

54. No one shall be arrested or imprisoned upon the appeal of a woman, for the death of any other than her husband.

55. All fines made with us unjustly and against the law of the land, and all amercements imposed unjustly and against the law of the land, shall be entirely remitted, or else it shall be done concerning them according to the decision of the five-and-twenty barons of whom mention is made below in the clause for securing the peace, or according to the judgment of the majority of the same, along with the aforesaid Stephen, archbishop of Canterbury, if he can be present, and such others as he may wish to bring with him for this purpose, and if he cannot be present the business shall nevertheless proceed without him, provided always that if any one or more of the aforesaid five-and-twenty barons are in a similar suit, they shall be removed as far as concerns this particular judgment, others being substituted in their places after having been selected by the rest of the same five-and-twenty for this purpose only, and after having been sworn.

56. If we have disseised or removed Welshmen from lands or liberties, or other things, without the legal judgment of their peers

in England or in Wales, they shall be immedately restored to them; and if a dispute arise over this, then let it be decided in the marches by the judgment of their peers; for tenements in England according to the law of England, for tenements in Wales according to the law of Wales, and for tenements in the marches according to the law of the marches. Welshmen shall do the same to us and ours.

57. Further, for all those possessions from which any Welshman has, without the lawful judgment of his peers, been disseised or removed by King Henry our father, or King Richard our brother, and which we retain in our hand (or which are possessed by others, to whom we are bound to warrant them) we shall have respite until the usual term of crusaders; excepting those things about which a plea has been raised or an inquest made by our order before we took the cross; but as soon as we return, (or if perchance we desist from our expedition), we will immediately grant full justice in accordance with the laws of the Welsh and in relation to the foresaid regions.

58. We will immediately give up the son of Llywelyn and all the hostages of Wales, and the charters delivered to us as security for the peace.

59. We will do toward Alexander, King of Scots, concerning the return of his sisters and his hostages, and concerning his franchises, and his right, in the same manner as we shall do towards our other barons of England, unless it ought to be otherwise according to the charters which we hold from William his father, formerly King of Scots; and this shall be according to the judgment of his peers in our court.

60. Moreover, all the aforesaid customs and liberties, the observance of which we have granted in our kingdom as far as pertains to us towards our men, shall be observed by all of our kingdom, as well clergy as laymen, as far as pertains to them towards their men.

61. Since, moreover, for God and the amendment of our kingdom, and for the better allaying of the quarrel that has arisen between us and our barons, we have granted all these concessions, desirous that they should enjoy them in complete and firm endurance forever, we give and grant to them the underwritten security, namely, that the barons choose five-and-twenty barons of the kingdom, whomsoever they will, who shall be bound with all their might, to observe

and hold, and cause to be observed, the peace and liberties we have
granted and confirmed to them by this our present Charter, so that
if we, or our justiciar, or our bailiffs or any one of our officers, shall
in anything be at fault toward anyone, or shall have broken any
one of the articles of the peace or of this security, and the offence
be notified to four barons of the aforesaid five-and-twenty, the
said four barons shall repair to us (or our justiciar, if we are out of
the realm) and, laying the transgression before us, petition to have
that transgression corrected without delay. And if we shall not have
corrected the transgression (or, in the event of our being out of
the realm, if our justiciar shall not have corrected it) within forty
days, reckoning from the time it has been intimated to us (or to our
justiciar, if we should be out of the realm), the four barons aforesaid shall refer that matter to the rest of the five-and-twenty barons,
and those five-and-twenty barons shall, together with the community
of the whole land, distrain and distress us in all possible ways,
namely, by seizing our castles, lands, possessions, and in any other
way they can, until redress has been obtained as they deem fit, saving
harmless our own person, and the persons of our queen and children; and when redress has been obtained, they shall resume their
old relations towards us. And let whoever in the country desires it,
swear to obey the orders of the said five-and-twenty barons for the
execution of all the aforesaid matters, and along with them, to
molest us to the utmost of his power; and we publicly and freely
grant leave to every one who wishes to swear, and we shall never
forbid anyone to swear. All those, moreover, in the land who of
themselves and of their own accord are unwilling to swear to the
twenty-five to help them in constraining and molesting us, we shall
by our command compel the same to swear to the effect foresaid. And
if any one of the five-and-twenty barons shall have died or departed
from the land, or be incapacitated in any other manner which
would prevent the foresaid provisions being carried out, those of
the said twenty-five barons who are left shall choose another in his
place according to their own judgment, and he shall be sworn in
the same way as the others. Further, in all matters the execution of
which is entrusted to these twenty-five barons, if perchance these
twenty-five are present and disagree about anything, or if some of
them, after being summoned, are unwilling or unable to be present,
that which the majority of those present ordain or command shall

be held as fixed and established, exactly as if the whole twenty-five had concurred in this; and the said twenty-five shall swear that they will faithfully observe all that is aforesaid, and cause it to be observed with all their might. And we shall procure nothing from anyone, directly or indirectly, whereby any part of these concessions and liberties might be revoked or diminished; and if any such thing has been procured, let it be void and null, and we shall never use it personally or by another.

62. And all the ill-will, hatreds, and bitterness that have arisen between us and our men, clergy and lay, from the date of the quarrel, we have completely remitted and pardoned to everyone. Moreover, all trespasses occasioned by the said quarrel, from Easter in the sixteenth year of our reign till the restoration of peace, we have fully remitted to all, both clergy and laymen, and completely forgiven, as far as pertains to us. And, on this head, we have caused to be made out to them letters patent of Stephen, archbishop of Canterbury, Henry, archbishop of Dublin, the bishops aforesaid, and master Pandulf, as evidences of this clause of security and of the foresaid concessions.

63. Wherefore it is our will, and we firmly enjoin, that the English Church be free, and that the men in our kingdom have and hold all the aforesaid liberties, rights, and concessions, well and peaceably, freely and quietly, fully and wholly, for themselves and their heirs, of us and our heirs, in all respects and in all places for ever, as is aforesaid. An oath, moreover, has been taken, as well on our part as on the part of the barons, that all these conditions aforesaid shall be kept in good faith and without evil intent. Given under our hand—the above-named and many others being witnesses—in the meadow which is called Runnymede, between Windsor and Staines, on the fifteenth day of June in the seventeenth year of our reign.

First Charter of Henry III, Reissue of Magna Carta, 1216 (substantially the same as Magna Carta, omitting arts. 10, 11, 12, 14, 15, 25, 27, 42, 45, 48–53, 57–9, and those after 60).

Bracton, *De legibus et consuetudinibus Angliae*,[7] between 1250 and 1258 (i, 1, 1 [fol. 1] i, 8, 5 [fol. 6]. Translated from the Tuttle text, 1640).

1. In a king who rules rightly these two things are necessary,

7. *On the Laws and Customs of England.*

namely, arms and laws, by which each time, of war and of peace, may be rightly governed; for each of these needs the help of the other whereby as well military affairs may be in safety as the laws themselves may be made secure by the use and protection of arms.

5. . . . Moreover, the king himself ought not to be under a man but under God and under the law, because the law makes the king. Therefore let the king attribute to the law what the law attributes to the king, namely, lordship and power, for there is no king where will governs and not law.

Confirmation of the Charters, by Edward I, 1297 (Stubbs' translation, *Select Charters and Other Illustrations of English Constitutional History*).

I. Edward, by the grace of God, King of England, Lord of Ireland, and Duke of Aquitaine, to all those that these present letters shall hear or see, greeting. Know ye that we to the honour of God and of holy Church, and to the profit of all our realm, have granted for us and our heirs, that the Great Charter of Liberties and the Charter of the Forest, which were made by common assent of all the realm, in the time of King Henry our father, shall be kept in every point without breach. And we will that these same charters shall be sent under our seal to our justices, both to those of the forest and to the rest, and to all sheriffs of shires, and to all our other officers, and to all our cities throughout the realm, together with our writs in the which it shall be contained, that they cause the aforesaid charters to be published, and have it declared to the people that we have granted that they shall be observed in all points, and that our justices, sheriffs, mayors, and other officials which under us have to administer the laws of our land, shall allow the said charters in pleas before them and in judgments in all their points; that is to wit, the Great Charter as the common law and the Charter of the Forest according to the Assize of the Forest, for the relief of our people.

II. And we will that if any judgment be given from henceforth, contrary to the points of the charters aforesaid, by the justices or by any other our ministers that hold plea before them against the points of the charters, it shall be undone and holden for naught.

III. And we will that the same charters shall be sent under our seal to cathedral churches throughout our realm, and there remain, and shall be read before the people twice in the year.

IV. And that archbishops and bishops shall pronounce sentences of greater excommunication against all those that by word, deed, or counsel shall go against the foresaid charters, or that in any point break or go against them. And that the said curses be twice a year denounced and published by the prelates aforesaid. And if the same prelates or any of them be remiss in the denunciation of the said sentences, the Archbishops of Canterbury and York for the time being, as is fitting, shall reprove them and constrain them to make that denunciation in form aforesaid.

V. And for so much as divers people of our realm are in fear that the aids and mises [8] which they have given to us beforetime towards our wars and other businesses, of their own grant and goodwill, however they were made, might turn to a bondage to them and their heirs, because they might be at another time found in the rolls, and so likewise the prises [9] taken throughout the realm by our ministers in our name: we have granted for us and our heirs, that we shall never draw such aids, mises, nor prises into a custom for anything that hath been done heretofore or that may be found by roll or in any other manner.

VI. Moreover, we have granted for us and our heirs, as well to archbishops, bishops, abbots, priors, and other folk of holy Church, as also to earls, barons, and to all the community of the land, that for no business from henceforth will we take such manner of aids, mises, nor prises from our realm, but by the common assent of all the realm, and for the common profit thereof, saving the ancient aids and prises due and accustomed.

VII. And for so much as the more part of the community of the realm find themselves sore grieved with the maletote on wools, that is to wit, a toll of forty shillings for every sack of wool, and have made petition to us to release the same; we, at their requests, have fully released it, and have granted that we shall never take this nor any other without their common assent and goodwill; saving to us and our heirs the custom of wools, skins, and leather granted before by the commonalty aforesaid. In witness of which things we have caused to be made these our letters patent.

8. Expenses.
9. Seizures of goods for the king's use.

Anonymous Case, Court of King's Bench, 1338 (Y.B. Mich. 12 Edw. III, no. 23. Pike's translation).

In a replevin where the defendant avowed the distress [i.e. seizure of property] for the cause that he was made collector of the fifteenths, etc., and did not show a warrant. Whereupon the plaintiff demanded judgment whether he ought to be received to that avowry without a specialty.[1] It was said that he was sub-collector and had to make an oath, and that he would not have any other warrant. Shareshull (J.) said that he could not by law be driven to act in that capacity without a special warrant, and that if he were arrested on that account, he would have a writ of false imprisonment.

Reginald De Nerford's Case, Court of King's Bench, 1339-40 (Y.B. Hil. 14 Edw. III, no. 34. Pike's translation).

Note. Reginald de Nerford and others were convicted as disseisors with force and arms wherefore an *exegi facias* [2] issued, which writ the sheriff returned to the effect that the king had instructed him by letter under the Targe that he had pardoned them their trespasses and the imprisonment, and commanded that they should not be put to damage on that account, and so by reason of the king's message he had done nothing, and he returned the king's letter.

Willoughby, J.: The letter should have been sent to us, and then we should have commanded the sheriff to stay proceedings; but the sheriff could not legally by virtue of any such letter have stayed proceedings otherwise than by warrant from the same place from which he had the order to outlaw. Wherefore the sheriff was in mercy [i.e. was fined] and a fresh *exegi facias* issued.

Decretum of Gratian,[3] Pars I, Distinctio X, canons 1, 4 (about 1150).

1. A law of the emperors cannot abrogate ecclesiastical rights. Of which Pope Nicholas [I, d. 867] writes to the bishops assembled in a council at Convicinum a law of the emperors is not to be used in any ecclesiastical controversies, especially since they are found at times to run counter to the evangelical and canonical sanction. A

1. Instrument under seal.
2. "Cause to be required." A writ to outlaw a person for not appearing in court to answer a summons.
3. The first part of the Corpus Iuris Canonici (Body of the Canon Law).

law of the emperors is not above the law of God but under it.
Ecclesiastical rights cannot be abrogated by an imperial judgment. . . .

4. Statutes cannot oppose good morals and the decrees of the
Roman pontiffs. Statutes contrary to the canons and decrees of the
Roman heads or against good morals are of no moment.

Decretals of Gregory IX, Lib. I, tit. 2, cap. 10 (a decretal of Innocent
III, 1199).

A general statute of the laity is not extended to churches or
ecclesiastical persons or their goods to their prejudice, nor a special
statute even if it involves their convenience and favor.

Lindwood, *Provinciale*,[4] ed. 1679, p. 263, note i (Lindwood died in
1446).

And note well that it says by royal assent, because such an ordinance made even in favor of the church by the mere motion of
the king and the two temporal estates would not be valid unless
so far as it was made at the requisition of the church or afterward
approved by the church.

Athon, *Constitutiones*,[5] ed. 1504, fol. 46 (constitution of Cardinal
Otho, Apostolic Legate, at a Pan-Anglican Council, 1236).

We command that diligent care be had as to the custody of seals,
so that each hold custody by himself or commits custody to one in
whose faith he confides, who shall swear that he faithfully guard
it and will not allow it to anyone for sealing of anything nor himself
seal anything whereby prejudice may arise to anyone unless the
master of it has first read and diligently looked into it and so has
commanded it to be sealed.

Rous v. the Abbot, Court of Common Pleas, 1450 (Statham, *Abridgment*, tit. Annuity).

One Rous brought a writ of annuity against an abbot and showed
a deed of the annuity made by the predecessor of the same abbot

4. Provincial Edict.
5. In the Roman law a *constitutio* is an enactment of the emperor.

and sealed with the convent seal and that the annuity was for certain loaves and beer and robes and other things, etc. Pole (Counsel for the defendant): "The Statute of Carlisle (35 Edw. I) willed that the Cistercians, Premonstratensians, and Austins, who have convent and common seal, that the common seal shall be in the custody of the Prior, who is under the Abbot, and of four others the wisest of the house, and that any deed sealed with the common seal that is not thus in custody shall be void. And we say at the time this deed was sealed the seal was out of their custody." And the opinion of the Court: That this statute is void, for it is impertinent to be observed, because the seal being in their custody the abbot cannot seal anything with it, but when it is in the hands of the abbot it is out of their custody *ipso facto*.[6] And if the statute should be observed every common seal will be defeated by a simple surmise that cannot be tried, etc. Note that it was well argued and that many exceptions were taken to the pleas, etc.

The Prior of Castleacre v. the Dean of St. Stephens, 1506 (Y.B. 21 Hen. VII, 1).

In a writ of annuity the case was this: The plaintiff made his title that all his predecessors had been seised of the annuity by the hands of one A, parson of the church of N and all his predecessors from time to which memory did not run until a certain year, etc., and that the annuity was in arrear, upon which he had brought his action. To which the defendant says that his parsonage is and had been appropriated to the Prior of B before time of memory, which is a cell of the Abbey of Caen in Normandy, and that King Edward III in time of war seised all the lands which were temporal lands of all the alien priors and so continued till Henry V. And in the second year of the latter's reign it was ordained by the authority of Parliament that "all the lands seised in the manner aforesaid remain in his possession to him and his successors forever," and so continued till King Edward IV, who by his letters patent (which he would show) granted the same parsonage to the defendant Dean of St. Stephen's to him and his successors forever, discharged as it was in his own hands.

Yaxley (counsel for plaintiff). It seems the action is maintainable because our title of prescription is affirmed. Accordingly during

6. "By that very fact."

the time in which the parsonage was in the hands of the King the annuity was in suspense because I cannot have my action against the King. . . . By this grant nothing was charged beyond the person of the parson and the persons of his successors, being parsons; and he must be charged by the name of parson. And the king was never parson although he had the parsonage. . . .

Butler (counsel for defendant) . . . By that act of Parliament by its very force it must be determined. For it is one of the highest records that there is in the law, and such a record that everyone in England is barred and shall be bound by it. Therefore when by the act aforesaid it was granted to the king and his heirs, by so much the annuity was determined. . . .

Kingsmill (Justice, interrupting). . . . But, sir, the act of Parliament cannot make the king to be parson, for we through our law cannot make any man to have spiritual jurisdiction; for nothing can do that but the supreme head. . . .

Coningsby (counsel for defendant) . . . The king has divers benefices in Wales, which are continually in his hands. . . .

(The case was ordered reargued. On reargument on another day:)

Palmes, one of the new Serjeants (counsel for plaintiff), stated the case as before and said that it seems first there are three things to consider: one, whether the parsonage was charged or only the parson; second, whether the act of Parliament could make the king a parson; third, whether, admitting that the king could be called parson, when he had granted out of his estate the annuity was revived. And, as to the first point, it seems that the parson only is charged and not the parsonage. For by a grant of annuity by a parson to another the glebe land is not charged, and this shows it well, that he (the grantee) shall not distrain for this rent nor shall he have an assize. And in case the king's tenant grants me for him and his heirs an annuity to me and my heirs and afterwards dies and the king seises, action for this annuity is maintainable against the heir notwithstanding the possession of the king; and this shows that the person is charged and not the land. Therefore here it seems that this annuity charges only the parson and not the parsonage. Through the act of Parliament it seems the King cannot be called parson, for no temporal act can make a temporal man have spiritual jurisdiction. For if it were ordained by act etc. that such a one should not offer tithes to his curate the act would be void, for of such thing as touches merely the spiritualty such temporal act can make no ordinance. The law is the same if it were enacted that one parson should have the tithes of another. So by this act, which is merely of a temporal court, the king cannot be made to have any spiritual jurisdiction. . .

Marow (counsel for defendant). . . . Then it is to be considered whether the king can have this spiritual possession, and it seems to me that he can: for if a parson grant me the tithes for a term of five years there is no question but I shall have them and still they are a spiritual thing, and if a parson leases me his benefice, I shall have it by force of the lease; so it is not inappropriate that a temporal man shall have spiritual things and therefore, as it seems to me, the king can have them. . . .

Fisher (Justice) rehearsed the case and said it seemed that the annuity still remained and the action was maintainable and that this annuity charges the person and the parsonage is not charged, but the person by force of the parsonage; for the annuity is only a personal thing. . . . And the king cannot be parson through this act of Parliament, nor can any temporal man through this act be called parson. . . .

Vavasour (Justice, dissenting): It seems to me the annuity is determined and the bar good. First to consider whether the king can be called a parson or not, and it seems to me that he can. And of this proposition I will put you many precedents. One, I know divers lords who have parsonages in their own use (and he gave their names and place certain); so it is not impertinent that the king should be called parson. . . . But this annuity, as it seems to me, is wholly extinguished by the act of Parliament, and this is the reason: The one who had the annuity is party to that act, so, although he had the right before the gift of the annuity by it, yet by that act, which is his own deed, and to which he is party, the annuity, etc. And it is as strong as if he had made a release: for if one has rent charge out of certain land and that land is by act of Parliament given to another person, I care not for I say that by that act of Parliament his rent is gone forever because he who had the rent was party to that act, since everyone in England is party to the act of Parliament. Because in the case here since he who had the annuity was party to that act it seems that by that act he shall be barred to claim it.

Frowick, Chief Justice, to the contrary: . . . Yaxley put a good case the other day, which was adjudged in 10 Henry V. And the case was that a parson brought writ of annuity against a Vicar and it was pleaded for the Vicar that the parson had entered on the vicarage before the writ was purchased, and this was held no plea because he remained vicar and the person of the Vicar is charged. And in the 11th year of Edward IV it was the opinion of all the justices that the parson only is charged. However I do not wish to dwell longer on this matter, but, as it seems to me, the parson is alone charged. As to the other matter, whether the King can be parson by the act of Parliament, as I understand it there is not much to argue. For I have not seen that any temporal man can be parson without the agreement of the Supreme Head. And in all the cases that have been put, namely, of the benefices in Wales and the benefices that laymen have to their own use, I have looked into the matter. The king had them by assent and agreement of the Supreme Head. So a temporal act, without the assent of the Supreme Head, cannot make the king parson.

Fortescue, *De laudibus legum Angliae*,[7] between 1467 and 1471 (chaps. ix, xxxiii–xxxvi. Amos' translation).

Chap. IX. The next thing, my Prince, at which you seem to hesitate, shall, with the same ease, be removed and answered, that is, whether you ought to apply yourself to the study of the *Laws of England*, or to that of the *Civil Laws*,[8] for that the opinion is with them every where, in preference to all other human laws: let not this difficulty, Sir! give you any concern. *A King of England cannot, at his pleasure, make any alterations in the laws of the land, for the nature of his government is not only regal, but political.* Had it been merely regal, he would have a power to make what innovations and alterations he pleased, in the laws of the kingdom, impose *tallages* and other hardships upon the people, whether they would or no, without their consent, which sort of government the *Civil Laws* point out, when they declare *Quod principi placuit legis habet*

7. *On Praises of the Laws of England.*
8. The Roman law which had been received in France.

vigorem: [9] but it is much otherwise with a king, whose government is *political,* because *he can neither make any alteration, or change in the laws of the realm without the consent of the subject, nor burthen them, against their wills, with strange impositions,* so that a people governed by such laws as are made by their own consent and approbation *enjoy their properties securely, and without the hazard of being deprived of them, either by the king or any other:* the same things may be effected under an *absolute prince,* provided he do not degenerate into the tyrant. Of such a prince, *Aristotle,* in the third of his *Politics,* says, "It is better for a city to be governed by a good man, than by good laws." But because it does not always happen, that the person presiding over a people, is so qualified, St. *Thomas,* in the book which he wrote to the king of *Cyprus,* (De Regimine Principum,) [1] *wishes, that a kingdom could be so instituted, as that the king might not be at liberty to tyrannize over his people; which only comes to pass* in the present case; that is, when the *sovereign power* is restrained by *political* laws.

Chap. XXXIII. Prince. I am convinced that the laws of England eminently excel, beyond the laws of all other countries, in the case you have been now endeavouring to explain; and yet I have heard that some of my ancestors, kings of England, have been so far from being pleased with those laws, that they have been industrious to introduce, and make the Civil Laws a part of the Constitution, in prejudice of the Common Law; this makes me wonder what they could intend by such behaviour.

Chap. XXXIV. Chancellor. You would cease to wonder, my Prince, if you would please seriously to consider the nature and occasion of the attempt. I have already given you to understand that there is a very noted sentence, a favourite maxim, or rule in the *Civil Law,* that, *That which pleases the Prince has the effect of a Law.* The Laws of England admit of no such maxim, or any thing like it. A King of England does not bear such a sway over his subjects, as a King *merely,* but in a *mixed political capacity:* he is obliged by his Coronation Oath to the observance of the laws, which some of our kings have not been well able to digest, because thereby

9. "The will of the emperor has the force of a law." Institutes of Justinian, 1, 2, 6 (A.D. 533).
1. "On the Government of Rulers."

they are deprived of that free exercise of dominion over their subjects, in that full extensive manner, as *those kings* have, *who* preside
and govern by an *absolute regal power;* who, in pursuance of the
laws of their respective kingdoms, in particular *the Civil Law,* and
of the aforesaid *maxim,* govern their subjects, change laws, enact
new ones, inflict punishments, and impose taxes, at their mere will
and pleasure, and determine suits at law in such manner, when,
and as they think fit. For which reason *your ancestors* endeavoured
to shake off this *political* frame of government, in order to exercise
the same *absolute regal dominion* too over their subjects, or rather
to be at their full swing to act as they list: not considering, that
the power of both kings is really, and in effect equal, as is set forth
in my aforesaid treatise, *de Natura Legis Naturae,*[2] viz. that it is not
a restraint, but rather a liberty to govern a people by the just
regularity of a *political* government, or rather right reason; that it
is the greatest security both to king and people, and takes off no
inconsiderable part of his royal care. That this may the better appear, you will please to consult the experience you have had of both
kinds of government; to begin with the *regal,* such as the king of
France exercises *at present* over his subjects; and, in the next place,
you will please to consider the effect of that *regal political government* which kings of *England* exercise over their subjects.

Chap. XXXV. You may remember, most worthy Prince, in what a
condition you observed the villages and towns of France to be
during the time you sojourned there. Though they were well
supplied with all the fruits of the earth, yet they were so much oppressed by the king's troops, and their horses; that you could scarce
be accommodated, in your travels, not even in the great towns:
where, as you were informed by the inhabitants, the soldiers, though
quartered in the same village a month or two, yet they neither did
nor would pay any thing for themselves or horses; and, what is still
worse, the inhabitants of the villages and towns where they came,
were forced to provide for them *gratis,* wines, flesh, and whatever
else they had occasion for; and if they did not like what they found,
the inhabitants were obliged to supply them with better from the
neighbouring villages: upon any non-compliance, the soldiers treated
them at such a barbarous rate, that they were quickly necessitated
to gratify them. When provisions, fuel and horse meat fell short

2. *On the Nature of Natural Law.*

in one village, they marched away full speed to the next; wasting it in like manner. They usurp and claim the same privilege and custom not to pay a penny for necessaries, either for themselves or women (whom they always carry with them in great numbers) such as shoes, stockings, and other wearing apparel, even to the smallest trifle of a lace, or point; all the inhabitants, wherever the soldiers quarter, are liable to this cruel oppressive treatment: it is the same throughout all the villages and towns in the kingdom, which are not walled. There is not any the least village, but what is exposed to the calamity, and once or twice in the year is sure to be plundered in this vexatious manner. Further, the king of France does not permit any one to use salt, but what is bought of himself, at his own arbitrary price: and, if any poor person would rather choose to eat his meat without salt, than to buy it at such an exorbitant dear rate: he is notwithstanding compellable to provide himself with salt, upon the terms aforesaid, proportionably to what shall be adjudged sufficient to subsist the number of persons he has in family: besides all this, the inhabitants of France give every year to their king the fourth part of all their wines, the growth of that year, every vintner gives the fourth penny of what he makes of his wines by sale. And all the towns and boroughs pay to the king yearly, great sums of money, which are assessed upon them for the expenses of his men at arms. So that the king's troops which are always considerable, are subsisted and paid yearly by those common people, who live in the villages, boroughs and cities. Another grievance is, every village constantly finds and maintains two cross-bow-men at the least; some find more well arrayed in all their accoutrements, to serve the king in his wars, as often as he pleaseth to call them out; which is frequently done. Without any consideration had of these things, other very heavy taxes are assessed yearly upon every village within the kingdom for the king's service; neither is there ever any intermission or abatement of taxes. Exposed to these and other calamities, the peasants live in great hardship and misery. Their constant drink is water, neither do they taste, throughout the year, any other liquor; unless upon some extraordinary times, or festival days. Their clothing consists of frocks, or little short jerkins made of canvass no better than common sackcloth; they do not wear any woollens, except of the coarsest sort; and that only in the garment under their frocks; nor do they wear

any trowse, but from the knees upward; their legs being exposed
and naked. The women go barefoot, except on holidays: they do
not eat flesh, unless it be the fat of bacon, and that in very small
quantities, with which they make a soup: of other sorts, either
boiled or roasted, they do not so much as taste, unless it be of the
inwards and offals of sheep and bullocks, and the like, which are
killed for the use of the better sort of people, and the merchants:
for whom also quails, partridges, hares, and the like, are reserved,
upon pain of the gallies: as for their poultry, the soldiers consume
them, so that scarce the eggs, slight as they are, are indulged them
by way of a dainty. And if it happen that a man is observed to
thrive in the world, and become rich, he is presently assessed to the
king's tax, proportionably more than his poorer neighbours, whereby
he is soon reduced to a level with the rest. This, or I am very much
mistaken, is the present state and condition of the peasantry of
France. The nobility and gentry are not so much burthened with
taxes. But if any one of them be impeached for a state-crime, though
by his known enemy, it is not usual to convene him before the ordinary judge, but he is very often examined in the king's own
apartment, or some such private place; sometimes only by the king's
pursuivants and messengers: as soon as the king, upon such information, shall adjudge him to be guilty, he is never more heard of;
but immediately, without any other formal process, the person so
accused and adjudged guilty is put into a sack, and by night thrown
into the river by the officers of the provost-marshal, and there
drowned: in which summary way, you have heard of more put to
death, than by any legal process. But still according to the Civil
Law, "what pleases the prince has the effect of a law." Other things
of a like irregular nature, or even worse, are well known to you,
during your abode in France, and the adjacent countries; acted
in the most detestable barbarous manner, under no colour or
pretext of law than what I have already declared. To be particular
would draw out our discourse into too great a length. Now it
remains to consider what effect that political mixed government,
which prevails in England, has, which some of your progenitors
have endeavoured to abrogate, and instead thereof to introduce the
Civil Law; that, from the consideration of both, you may certainly
determine with yourself which is the more eligible, since (as is
above-mentioned) the philosopher says, "that opposites laid one by

the other, do more certainly appear;" or, as more to our present argument, "happinesses by their contraries are best illustrated."

Chap. XXXVI. In England no one takes up his abode in another man's house, without leave of the owner first had: unless it be in public inns; and there he is obliged to discharge his reckoning, and make full satisfaction, for what accommodations he has had, ere he be permitted to depart. Neither is it lawful to take away another man's goods without the consent of the proprietor, or being liable to be called to an account for it. No man is concluded, but that he may provide himself with salt, and other necessaries for his family, when, how and where he pleases. Indeed the king, by his purveyors, may take for his own use necessaries for his household, at a reasonable price, to be assessed at the discretion of the constables of the place, whether the owners will or not: but the king is obliged by the laws to make present payment, or at a day to be fixed by the great officers of the king's household. The king cannot despoil the subject, without making ample satisfaction for the same: He cannot by himself, or his ministry, lay taxes, subsidies, or any imposition, of what kind soever, upon the subject; he cannot alter the laws, or make new ones, without the express consent of the whole kingdom in Parliament assembled: every inhabitant is at his liberty fully to use and enjoy whatever his farm produceth, the fruits of the earth, the increase of his flock, and the like: all the improvements he makes, whether by his own proper industry, or of those he retains in his service, are his own to use and enjoy without the lett, interruption, or denial of any: if he be in any wise injured, or oppressed, he shall have his amends and satisfaction against the party offending: hence it is, that the inhabitants are rich in gold, silver, and in all the necessaries and conveniences of life. They drink no water, unless at certain times, upon a religious score, and by way of doing penance. They are fed, in great abundance, with all sorts of flesh and fish, of which they have plenty everywhere; they are clothed throughout in good woollens; their bedding and other furniture in their houses are of wool, and that in great store: they are also well provided with all other sorts of household goods and necessary implements for husbandry: every one, according to his rank, hath all things which conduce to make life easy and happy. They are not sued at law but before the ordinary judge, where they are treated with mercy and justice, according to the laws of the land; neither are they impleaded in point of property, or arraigned for any capital crime, how heinous soever, but before the king's judges, and according to the laws of the land. These are the advantages consequent from that political mixed government which obtains in England: from hence it is plain, what the effects of that law are in practice, which some of your ancestors, kings of England, have endeavoured to abrogate: the effects of that other law are no less apparent, which they so zealously endeavoured to introduce among us; so that you may easily distinguish them by their comparative advantages; what then could induce those kings to endeavour such an alteration, but only ambition, luxury, and impotent passion, which they preferred to the good of the State. You will please to consider in the next place, my good Prince, some other matters which will follow to be treated of.

Matter of Cavendish, Common Pleas, 1587 (1 Anderson, 152. Thayer's translation).

One R. Cavendish suggested to the queen that she had power to establish the office of making all the writs of *supersedeas quia improvide emanavit* [3] in the Common Bench: whereupon the queen, by her letters-patent, granted to the said Cavendish the office of making the said writs for some years, with words of *constituimus;* [4] after making which patent, the judges were commanded orally, by a messenger, to admit the said Cavendish to the said office. The judges did not do it; and thereupon Cavendish procured the directing of a letter to the said judges, under the sign-manual and signet, in these words:—

"We let you weet that our express will and commandment is, that forthwith you give order that a sequestration of all the profits already grown since our grant to our said servant, and continuing to grow of the said office, be made and committed unto such persons as you shall think meet, with whom you shall take order by bond or other sufficient manner to answer, and yield the same profits unto our said servant, or to any other to whom the same shall be due immediately after the controversy for the execution of the said office shall be decided or ordered, whereof we eftsoones will you not to fail, &c."

3. "Supersede because it issued improvidently."
4. "We ordain."

The justices considered this letter, and thought that they could not lawfully act according to the contents of the said letter and its order, because it might be that by such sequestration others, alleging the right to make these writs, might be disseised of their freehold, claimed by them, in the making of these writs and fees thereupon. All this was told the queen by great men, friends of Cavendish. Thereupon another letter, under the signet and sign-manual, was directed to the justices, as follows:—

"Our will and pleasure is, and thereunto we will and command you that upon our said servant offering of himself unto you in our said court this next term, you presently without any further delay admit him unto the use, execution, and profits of the said office according to our said grant; for that we be nothing ignorant that if any of your clerks have any such title or interest as they pretend, both our laws lie open for their remedy, and also they be persons both for wealth and skill able to recover their own right if any such be. In consideration whereof we look that you and every of you should dutifully fulfil our commandment therein, and these our letters shall be your warrant, &c."

This letter was delivered to the justices in presence of the Lord Chancellor of England and the Earl of Leicester at the beginning of the Easter Term, in the twenty-ninth year of the queen (1587); and the Lord Chancellor declared to the judges that the queen had made the said patent to Cavendish upon a great desire that she had to provide advancement for him; that she understood that by this means he might enjoy this (right), and that she cared much about it. On which account she had commanded him and the said vis-count (sic) to hear the answer of the justices to the contents of the letter last mentioned. Thereupon the justices took the letter, and desired a little time to inspect and consider it; which was thought convenient. After perusing the letter, they went at once to the said lords and said for their answer that in all lawful points they would dutifully and in humble manner obey her Majesty, but as regards this case they could not without being perjured; and this, as they said, they well knew that the queen would not knowingly command or require.

Upon this they departed; and the said answer was reported to the queen, who commanded the said Chancellor, the Chief Justice of the King's Bench, and the Master of the Rolls to hear from the said judges the reasons and grounds which moved them to make such an answer; and also what they had to say against the prerogative and right of the queen in this matter; and therewith the learned counsel of the queen were commanded to attend. All these being assembled, the queen's sergeant showed that the queen had the right and prerogative of granting the making of these writs. . . . To which, for the judges, it was protested that with all their power they would aid her Majesty in all her rights, being bound thereto not only by common duty, but by oath, which rights they wished might be maintained and preserved; but for their answer it was said that this mode of proceeding was out of the course of justice, and therefore they would not make answer to those who had spoken. Their reasons they gave as follows, viz.: that they had and claimed nothing as to the making of the said writs, but the prenotaries and diverse exigenters of the same place,—who claimed it as a freehold for their lives. These, in law and reason, should be brought to answer, and not the judges; for these, and no others, were they who were to be touched as regards profit or damage by this; and always they who have the thing in controversy are the persons to answer as to what is in question. On this point no other answer was made.

When this was ended, the letters above recited were shown, and the judges were charged with not having obeyed the orders therein contained. To this they said that they must needs confess that they had not performed the orders; but this was no offence or contempt to her Majesty, for the orders were against the law of the land (*le ley de terre*),[5] in which case it was said, no one is bound to obey such an order: and they offered to show what had been adjudged heretofore to prove what they said to be true.

And they said that the queen herself was sworn and took oath to keep her laws, and the judges also, as regards their willingly breaking them. As to this matter, so far as it concerned the judges, they answered again that if they obeyed these orders they should act otherwise than the laws warranted, and merely and directly against them; and that was contrary to their oath, and in contempt of God, her Majesty, and the country and commonwealth in which they were born and lived; of which, if the fear of God were gone from them, yet the examples of others and the punishment of those who had

5. Law French: "the law of the land."

formerly violated the laws, reminded them, and recalled them from such offences. The examples and precedents in these matters were remembered; namely: (Then followed brief statements as to Hugh Despenser, Lord Chamberlain of Edward II., Thorp, J., in the time of Edward III., "certain precedents of the time of Richard II.," and last the indictments against Empson, lately councillor to King Henry VII.; one of which only is recited at large, *pur avoyder tediusness*.[6] Then Magna Carta, c. 29 (9H. III.) was cited, and statutes 5 Ed. III. c. 9, and 28 Ed. III. c. 3; and another of 11 Rich., providing "that neither letters of signet, nor of the King's secret seal, shall be from henceforth sent in damage or prejudice of the realm.")

By which laws the office and duty of judges appears and of all others whomsoever; and also by the precedents before cited it appears what an offence it is willingly to break the laws of the land. . . . For these reasons, and because the queen and the judges are sworn, they said that they would not act according to the said letters. The oath of the queen and the judges appears in print, and so it need not be written here.

All this was reported by the said Lord Chancellor to the queen with his good allowance of the matters aforsaid and reasons alleged; which her Majesty, as I have heard, well accepted. But nothing more was done or heard by the judges in the said Easter Term, or in the Trinity Term then next following; which moves the judges to think that no more will ever be.

Darcy v. Allen, King's Bench, 1603 (Moore, 671, 11 Co. 84b. Thayer's version from Moore and Coke).

In the King's Bench; an action on the case; and a count that, whereas men of mean trades and occupations in the commonwealth apply themselves to idle games with cards, the queen, by way of redress and restraint of this enormity, made letters-patent to Ralph Bowes, authorizing him and his factors and deputies to provide playing-cards and prohibiting all others to import playing-cards into the realm or to make or sell them in the realm for a certain term

---

6. "In order to avoid tediousness." Law French, the language of the reports and texts down to the seventeenth century. It had long ceased to be spoken and writers who could not recall the French word wrote in the English word they meant.

of years now expired, and (reciting the grant) she made another like grant to Darcy, who provided cards accordingly: yet the defendant brought cards into the realm and sold them and did things contrary to the privilege granted to the plaintiff, and to his damage to the amount of £2,000. The defendant pleaded the custom of London, that a freeman may buy and sell all things merchantable, and that, since he was a freeman and haberdasher of London, and cards were things merchantable, he bought and sold them; and he demanded judgment. The plaintiff demurred in law; and it was argued first, Trin. 44 Eliz. (1602), by Altham, with the plaintiff, and Dyer, with the defendant. . . . Afterwards, Mich. 44 and 45 Eliz. (1602), it was argued by Dodderidge, against the patent, and by Fleming, solicitor, with the patent; and afterwards, the same term, by Fuller, against the patent, and Coke, Attorney-General, with the patent. And Dodderidge said that the case was tender, concerning the prince's prerogative and the subject's liberty, and must be argued with much caution; for he that hews above his head chips will fall into his eyes, and *qui majestatem scrutatur principis opprimetur splendore ejus.*[7] Yet since it is the honor and safety of the prince to govern by the laws, . . . as Bracton says, *merito retribuat Rex legi quod lex attribuat ei,*[8] therefore the princes of this realm have always been content that their patents and grants should be examined by the laws, and so is her Majesty that now is. In this examination it has always been held by the judges that the queen's grants procured against the usual and settled liberty of the subjects are void, and also those which tend to their grievance and oppression. . . .

It was . . . resolved by Popham, Chief Justice, *et per totam curiam,*[9] that the said grant to the plaintiff of the sole making of cards within the realm was utterly void, and that for two reasons: 1. That it is a monopoly, and against the common law. 2. That it is against divers Acts of Parliament. . . .

3. The queen was deceived in her grant; for the queen, as by the preamble appears, intended it to be for the weal public, and it will be employed for the private gain of the patentee, and for the prejudice of the weal public; moreover the queen meant that the abuse should be taken away, which shall never be by this patent,

7. "One who examines thoroughly the majesty of the king is oppressed by its splendor."
8. "The king justly returns to the law what the law attributes to him."
9. "And by the whole court."

but *potius* [1] the abuse will be increased for the private benefit of the patentee, and therefore, as it is said in 21 E. 3, 47, in the Earl of Kent's case, this grant is void *jure Regio*.[2] 4. This grant is *primae impressionis*,[3] for no such was ever seen to pass by letters-patent under the great seal before these days, and therefore it is a dangerous innovation, as well without any precedent, or example, as without authority or law or reason. . . . And therefore it was resolved, that the queen could not suppress the making of cards within the realm, no more than the making of dice, bowls, balls, hawks' hoods, bells, lures, dog-couples, and other the like, which are works of labor and art, although they serve for pleasure, recreation, and pastime, and cannot be suppressed but by Parliament, nor a man restrained from exercising any trade, but by Parliament, 37 E. 3, cap. 16, 5 Eliz. cap. 4 . . .

Also such charter of a monopoly, against the freedom of trade and traffic, is against divers Acts of Parliament, sc. 9 E. 3, c. 1 & 2, which for the advancement of the freedom of trade and traffic extends to all things vendible, notwithstanding any charter of franchise granted to the contrary, or usage, or custom, or judgment given upon such charter, which charters are adjudged by the same Parliament to be of no force or effect, and made to the derogation of the prelates, earls, barons, and grandees of the realm, and to the oppression of the Commons. And by the statute of 25 E. 3, cap. 2, it is enacted that the said Act of 9 E. 3, shall be observed, holden, and maintained in all points. And it is further by the same Act provided, that if any statute, charter, letters-patent, proclamation, command, usage, allowance, or judgment be made to the contrary, that it shall be utterly void. *Vide Magna Charta*, cap. 18, 27 E. 3 cap. 11, &c. . . .

And *nota*, reader, and well observe the glorious preamble and pretence of this odious monopoly. And it is true *quod privilegia quae re vera sunt in praejudicium reipublicae, magis tamen speciosa habent frontispicia, et boni publici praetextum, quam bonae et legales concessiones, sed praetextu liciti non debet admitti illicitum.*[4] And our lord the king that now is, in a book which he in zeal to

1. "Rather."
2. "As a matter of royal right."
3. "Of first impression."
4. "That privileges which are in truth in prejudice of the Commonwealth nevertheless have more specious frontispieces and pretext of public good than good and legal concessions; but pretext of the licit ought not to admit the illicit.

the law and justice commanded to be printed anno 1610, entitled, "A Declaration of His Majesty's Pleasure, &c.," p. 13, has published, that monopolies are things against the laws of this realm, and therefore expressly commands that no suitor presume to move him to grant any of them, &c.

Extracts from Coke's *Second Institute*. Commentary on Magna Carta, published 1642 by order of the House of Commons.

On chap. 29. This chapter containeth nine severall branches.

1. That no man be taken or imprisoned, but *per legem terrae*,[5] that is, by the common law, statute law, or custome of England; for these words, *per legem terrae*, being towards the end of this chapter, doe referre to all the precedent matters in this chapter, and this hath the first place, because the liberty of a mans person is more precious to him, than all the rest that follow, and therefore it is great reason, that he should by law be relieved therein, if he be wronged, as hereafter shall be shewed.

2. No man shall be disseised, that is, put out of seisin, or dispossessed of his free-hold (that is) lands, or livelihood, or of his liberties, or free-customes, that is, of such franchises, and freedomes, and free-customes, as belong to him by his free birth right, unlesse it be by the lawfull judgement, that is, verdict of his equals (that is, of men of his own condition) or by the law of the land (that is, to speak it once for all) by the due course, and processe of law.

3. No man shall be out-lawed, made an *exlex*,[6] put out of the law, that is, deprived of the benefit of the law, unlesse he be outlawed according to the law of the land.

4. No man shall be exiled, or banished out of his country, that is *nemo perdet patriam*,[7] no man shall lose his country, unlesse he be exiled according to the law of the land.

5. No man shall be in any sort destroyed (*destruere, i. quod prius structum, et factum fuit, penitus evertere et diruere*)[8] unless it be by the verdict of his equals, or according to the law of the land.

6. No man shall be condemned at the kings suite, either before

5. "By the law of the land."
6. "Outlaw."
7. "No one shall lose his country."
8. "To destroy, that is, wholly to overturn and demolish what was before built and became fact."

the king in his bench, where the pleas are *coram rege* [9] (and so are the words, *nec super eum ibimus,*[1] to be understood) nor before any other commissioner, or judge whatsoever, and so are the words, *nec super eum mittemus,*[2] to be understood, but by the judgement of his peers, that is, equalls, or according to the law of the land.

7. We shall sell to no man justice or right.

8. We shall deny to no man justice or right.

9. We shall defer to no man justice or right.

The genuine sense being distinctly understood, we shall proceed in order to unfold how the same have been declared, and interpreted. 1. By authority of parliament. 2. By our books. 3. By precedent.

(3) *Nullus liber homo capiatur, aut imprisonetur.*) [3] Attached and arrested are comprehended herein.

No man shall be taken (that is) restrained of liberty, by petition. or suggestion, to the king, or to his councell, unlesse it be by indictment, or presentment of good, and lawfull men, where such deeds be done. This branch, and divers other parts of this act have been notably explained by divers acts of parliament, &c. quoted in the margent.

2. No man shall be disseised. &c.

Hereby is intended, that lands, tenements, goods, and chattells shall not be seised into the kings hands, contrary to this great charter, and the law of the land; nor any man shall be disseised of his lands, or tenements, or dispossessed of his goods, or chattels, contrary to the law of the land.

A custome was alledged in the town of C. that if the tenant cease by two yeares, that the lord should enter into the freehold of the tenant and hold the same untill he were satisfied of the arrerages, and it was adjudged a custom against the law of the land, to enter into a mans freehold in that case without action or answer.

King H. 6, graunted to the corporation of diers within London, power to search, &c. and if they found any cloth died with logwood, that the cloth should be forfeit: and it was adjudged, that this charter concerning the forfeiture, was against the law of the land,

9. "Before the king."
1. "Nor set forth against him."
2. "Nor send against him."
3. "No free man shall be taken or imprisoned."

and this statute: for no forfeiture can grow by letters patents.

No man ought to be put from his livelihood without answer.

3. No man outlawed, that is, barred to have the benefit of the law. Vide for the word, the first part of the Institutes.

Note to this word *utlagetur*,[4] these words, *nisi per legem terrae*,[5] do refer.

(4) *De libertatibus*.) [6] This word, *libertates*, liberties, hath three significations:

1. First, as it hath been said, it signifieth the laws of the realme, in which respect this charter is called *charta libertatum*.

2. It signifieth the freedomes, that the subjects of England have; for example, the company of the merchant tailors of England, having power by their charter to make ordinances, made an ordinance, that every brother of the same society should put the one half of his clothes to be dressed by some clothworker free of the same company, upon pain to forfeit x. s. &c, and it was adjudged that this ordinance was against law, because it was against the liberty of the subject, for every subject hath freedome to put his clothes to be dressed by whom he will, *et sic de similibus:* [7] and so it is, if such or the like graunt had been made by his letters patents.

3. Liberties signifieth the franchises, and priviledges, which the subjects have of the gift of the king, as the goods, and chattels of felons, outlawes, and the like, or which the subject claim by prescription, as wreck, waife, straie, and the like.

So likewise, and for the same reason, if a graunt be made to any man, to have the sole making of cards, or the sole dealing with any other trade, that graunt is against the liberty and freedome of the subject, that before did, or lawfully might have used that trade, and consequently against this great charter.

Generally all monopolies are against this great charter, because they are against the liberty and freedome of the subject, and against the law of the land.

4. No man exiled.

By the law of the land no man can be exiled, or banished out of his native countrey, but either by authority of parliament, or in

4. "Outlawed."
5. "Unless by the law of the land."
6. "Of liberties.
7. "And so in like cases."

case of abjuration for felony by the common law: and so when our books, or any record speak of exile, or banishment, other than in case of abjuration, it is to be intended to be done by authority of parliament: as Belknap and other judges, &c. banished into Ireland.

5. No man destroyed, &c.

That is, fore-judged of life, or limbe, disherited, or put to torture, or death.

Every oppression against law, by colour of any usurped authority is a kinde of destruction, for, *quando aliquid prohibetur, prohibetur et omne, per quod devenitur ad illud:* [8] and it is the worst oppression, that is done by colour of justice.

It is to be noted, that to this verb *destratur,*[9] are added *aliquo modo,*[1] and to no other verb in this chapter, and therefore all things, by any manner of meanes tending to destruction, are prohibited: as if a man be accused, or indicted of treason, or felony, his lands, or goods cannot be graunted to any, no not so much as by promise, nor any of his lands, or goods seised into the kings hands, before attainder: for when a subject obtaineth a promise of the forfeiture, many times undue meanes and more violent prosecution is used for private lucre, tending to destruction, than the quiet and just proceeding of law would permit, and the party ought to live of his own untill attainder.

(6) *Per judicium parium suorum.*) [2] By judgement of his peers Onely a lord of parliament of England shall be tried by his peers being lords of parliament: and neither noblemen of any other country, nor others that are called lords, and are no lords, of parliament, are accounted *pares,* peers within this statute.

Here note, as is before said, that this is to be understood of the kings sute for the words be, *nec super eum ibimus, nec super eum mittemus, nisi per legale judicium parium suorum.*[3] Therefore, for example, if a noble man be indicted for murder, he shall be tried by his peers, but if an appeale be brought against him, which is the suite of the party, there he shall not be tried by his peeres, but by

8. "When something is prohibited everything is also prohibited which comes down to it."

9. "Shall be destroyed."

1. "In any manner."

2. "By judgment of his peers."

3. Nor shall we set forth against him, nor send against him unless by legal judgment of his peers."

an ordinary jury of twelve men: and that for two reasons. First, for that the appeale cannot be brought before the lord high steward of England, who is the only judge of noble men, in case of treason, or felony. Secondly, this statute extendeth only to the kings suite.

And it extendeth to the kings suite in case of treason, or felony, or of misprision of treason, or felony, or being accessary to felony before, or after, and not to any other inferior offence. Also it extendeth to the triall itselfe, whereby he is to be convicted: but a nobleman is to be indicted of treason, or felony, or of misprision, or being accessary to, in case of felony, by an inquest under the degree of nobility: the number of the noble men that are to be triers are, 12. or more.

(7) *Per legale judicium.*) [4] By this word *legale,* amongst others, three things are implied. 1. That this manner of triall was by law, before this statute. 2. That their verdict must be legally given, wherein principally it is to be observed. 1. That the lords ought to heare no evidence, but in the presence, and hearing of the prisoner. 2. After the lords be gone together to consider of the evidence, they cannot send to the high steward to aske the judges any question of law, but in the hearing of the prisoner, that he may heare, whether the case be rightly put, for *de facto jus oritur;* [5] neither can the lords, when they are gone together, send for the judges to know any opinion in law, but the high steward ought to demand it in court in the hearing of the prisoner. 3. When all the evidence is given by the kings learned councell, the high steward cannot collect the evidence against the prisoner, or in any sort conferre with the lords touching their evidence, in the absence of the prisoner, but he ought to be called to it; and all this is implied in this word, *legale.* [6] And therefore it shall be necessary for all such prisoners, after evidence given against him, and before he depart from the barre, to require justice of the lord steward, and of the other lords, that no question be demanded by the lords, or speech or conference had by any with the lords, but in open court in his presence, and hearing, or else he shall not take any advantage thereof after verdict, and judgement given: but the handling thereof at large and of other

4. "By legal judgment."
5. "Law arises from fact."
6. "Legal."

things concerning this matter, belongs to another treatise, as before I have shewed, only this may suffice for the exposition of this statute.

And it is here called *judicium parium*,[7] and not *veredictum*,[8] because the noble men returned, and charged, are not sworne, but give their judgement upon their honour and ligeance to the king, for so are all the entries of record, separately beginning at the *puisne* lord, and so ascending upward.

And though of ancient time the lords, and peeres of the realme used in parliament to give judgement, in case of treason and felony, against those, that were no lords of parliament, yet at the suite of the lords it was enacted, that albeit the lords and peeres of the realme, as judges of the parliament, in the presence of the king, had taken upon them to give judgement, in case of treason and felony, of such as were no peeres of the realme, that hereafter no peeres shall be driven to give judgement on any others, then on their peeres according to the law.

(8) *Nisi per legem terrae*.) But by the law of the land. For the true sense and exposition of these words, see the statute of 37 E. 3 cap. 8 where the words, by the law of the land, are rendred without due proces of law, for there it is said, though it be contained in the great charter, that no man be taken, imprisoned, or put out of his free-hold without process of the law; that is, by indictment or presentment of good and lawfull men, where such deeds be done in due manner, or by writ originall of the common law.

Without being brought in to answere but by due proces of the common law.

No man be put to answer without presentment before justices, or thing of record, or by due proces, or by writ originall, according to the old law of the land.

Wherein it is to be observed, that this chapter is but declaratory of the old law of England. Rot. Parliament. 43 E. 3 nu. 22, 23. the case of Sir John a Lee, the steward of the kings house.

Per legem terrae.[9] i. *Per legem Angliae*,[1] and hereupon all commissions are grounded wherein is this clause, *facturi quod ad justitiam*

7. "Judgment by peers."
8. "Verdict.
9. "By the law of the land."
1. "That is by the law of England."

pertinet secundum legem, et consuetudinem Angliae,[2] &c. And it is not said, *legem et consuetudinem regis Angliae,*[3] lest it might be thought to bind the king only, nor *populi Angliae,*[4] lest it might be thought to bind them only, but that the law might extend to all, it is said *per legem terrae, i. Angliae.*[5]

And aptly it is said in this act, *per legem terrae,* that is, by the law of England: for into those places, where the law of England runneth not, other lawes are allowed in many cases, and not prohibited by this act. For example: if any injury, robbery, felony, or other offence be done upon the high sea, *lex terrae* [6] extendeth not to it, therefore the admirall hath conusance thereof, and may proceed, according to the marine law, by imprisonment of the body, and other proceedings, as have been allowed by the lawes of the realme.

Against this ancient, and fundamentall law, and in the face thereof, I finde an act of parliament made, that as well justices of assise, as justices of peace (without any finding or presentment by the verdict of twelve men) upon a bare information for the king before them made, should have full power, and authority by their discretions to heare, and determine all offences, and contempts committed, or done by any person, or persons against the forme, ordinance, and effect of any statute made, and not repealed, &c. By color of which act, shaking this fundamentall law, it is not credible what horrible oppressions, and exactions, to the undoing of infinite numbers of people, were committed by Sir Richard Empson knight, and Edm. Dudley being justices of peace, throughout England; and upon this unjust and injurious act (as commonly in like cases it falleth out) a new office was erected, and they made masters of the kings forfeitures.

But at the parliament, holden in the first yeare of H. 8. this act of 11 H. 7. is recited, and made voide, and repealed, and the reason is yeelded, for that by force of the said act, it was manifestly known, that many sinister, and crafty, feigned, and forged informations, had been pursued against divers of the kings subjects to their great dam-

2. "To do what pertains to justice according to the law and custom of England."

3. "Law and custom of the king of England."

4. "Of the people of England."

5. "By the law of the land, that is, of England."

6. "Law of the land."

mage, and wrongfull vexation: and the ill successe hereof, and the fearefull ends of these two oppressors, should deterre others from committing the like, and should admonish parliaments, that in stead of this ordinary, and pretious triall *per legem terrae,* they bring not in absolute, and partiall trialls by discretion.

If one be suspected for any crime, be it treason, felony, &c. And the party is to be examined upon certaine interrogatories, he may heare the interrogatories, and take a reasonable time to answer the same with deliberation (as there the time of deliberation was tenne houres) and the examinate, if he will, may put his answere in writing, and keepe a copy thereof: and so it was resolved in parliament by the lords spirituall and temporall, in the case of justice Richill. See the record at large.

Now here it is to be knowne, in what cases a man by the law of the land, may be taken, arrested, attached, or imprisoned in case of treason or felony, before presentment, indictment, &c. Wherein it is to be understood, that proces of law is two fold, viz. By the kings writ, or by due proceeding, the warrant, either in deed, or in law without writ.

As first, where there is any witnesse against the offendor, he may be taken and arrested by lawfull warrant, and committed to prison.

When treason and felony is committed, and the common fame and voice is, that A. is guilty, it is lawfull for any man, that suspects him, to apprehend him.

So it is of hue and cry, and that is by the statute of Winchester, which is but an affirmance of the common law: likewise if A. be suspected and he fleeth, or hideth himselfe, it is a good cause to arrest him.

If treason or felony be done, and one hath just cause of suspition, this is a good cause, and warrant in law, for him to arrest any man, but he must shew in certainty the cause of his suspition: and whether the suspition be just, or lawfull, shall be determined by the justices in an action of false imprisonment brought by the party grieved, or upon a *habeas corpus,*[7] &c.

A felony is done, and one is pursued upon hue and cry, that is not of ill fame, suspicious, unknown, nor indicted; he may be by a warrant in law, attached and imprisoned by the law of the land.

A watchman may arrest a night walker by a warrant in law.

7. "Have the body," i.e. bring the body of a person before the court.

If a man woundeth another dangerously, any man may arrest him by a warrant in law, until it may be known, whether the party wounded shall die thereof, or no.

If a man keep the company of a notorious thiefe, whereby he is suspected, &c. it is a good cause, and a warrant in law to arrest him.

If an affray be made to the breach of the kings peace, any man may by a warrant in law restrain any of the offenders, to the end the kings peace may be kept, but after the affray ended, they cannot be arrested without an expresse warrant.

Now seeing that no man can be taken, arrested, attached, or imprisoned but by due process of law, and according to the law of the land, these conclusions hereupon doe follow.

First, that a commitment by lawfull warrant, either in deed or in law, is accounted in law due processe or proceeding of law, and by the law of the land, as well as by processe by force of the kings writ.

2. That he or they, which doe commit them, have lawfull authority.

3. That his warrant, or *mittimus* [8] be lawfull, and that must be in writing under his hand and seale.

4. The cause must be contained in the warrant, as for treason, felony, &c. or for suspition of treason or felony, &c. otherwise if the mittimus contain no cause at all, if the prisoner escape, it is no offence at all, whereas if the mittimus contained the cause, the escape were treason, or felony, though he were not guilty of the offence; and therefore for the kings benefit, and that the prisoner may be the more safely kept, the mittimus ought to contain the cause.

5. The warrant or mittimus containing a lawfull cause, ought to have a lawfull conclusion, viz. and him safely to keep, untill he be delivered by law, &c. and not untill the party committing doth further order. And this doth evidently appeare by the writs of *habeas corpus,* both in the kings bench, and common pleas, eschequer and chancery.

The like writ is to be graunted out of the chancery, either in the time of the terme (as in the kings bench) or in the vacation; for

8. "We send." That is, the court or magistrate commits someone to be detained.

the court of chancery is *officina justitiae*,[9] and is ever open, and never adjourned, so as the subject being wrongfully imprisoned, may have justice for the liberty of his person as well in the vacation time as in the terme.

By these writs it manifestly appeareth, that no man ought to be imprisoned, but for some certain cause: and these words, *ad subjiciend. et recipiend.*[1] &c. prove that cause must be showed: for otherwise how can the court take order therein according to the law?

And this doeth agree with that which is said in the holy history *Sine ratione mihi videtur, mittere vinctum in carcerem, et causas ejus non significare.*[2] But since we wrote these things, and passed over to many other acts of parliament; see now the petition of right, *anno tertio Caroli regis,*[3] resolved in full parliament by the king, the lords spirituall, and temporall, and the commons, which hath made an end of this question, if any were.

Imprisonment doth not onely extend to false imprisonment, and unjust, but for detaining of the prisoner longer then he ought, where he was at the first lawfully imprisoned.

If the kings writ come to the sheriffe, to deliver the prisoner, if he detain him, this detaining is an imprisonment against the law of the land: if a man be in prison, a warrant cannot be made to the gaoler to deliver the prisoner to the custody of any person unknown to the gaoler, for two causes; first, for that thereby the kings writ of habeas corpus, or delivery, might be prevented. 2. The mittimus ought to bee, as hath beene said, till hee bee delivered by law.

If the sheriffe, or gaoler detain a prisoner in the gaole after his acquittall, unless it be for his fees, this is false imprisonment.

In many cases a man may be by the law of the land taken, and imprisoned, by force of the kings writ upon a suggestion made.

But if any man by colour of any authority, where he hath not any in that particular case, arrest, or imprison any man, or cause him to be arrested, or imprisoned, this is against this act, and it is most hatefull, when it is done by countenance of justice.

9. "Workshop of justice."
1. "To submit to and receive."
2. This is from the Vulgate of Acts 25:27. In the King James version: "For it seemeth to me unreasonable to send a prisoner and not withal to signify the crimes laid against him."
3. "In the third year of King Charles I."

King Edw. 6. did incorporate the town of S. Albons, and granted
to them to make ordinances, &c. they made an ordinance upon
paine of imprisonment, and it was adjudged to be against this
statute of Magna Charta; so it is, if such an ordinance had been contained in the patent it selfe.

All commissions that are consonant to this act, are, as hath been
said, *secundum legem, et consuetudinem Angliae.*[4]

A commission was made under the great seal to take I.N. (a
notorious felon) and to seise his lands, and goods: this was resolved
to be against the law of the land, unlesse he had been endicted, or
appealed by the party, or by other due processe of law.

It is enacted, if any man be arrested, or imprisoned against the
forme of this great charter, that he bee brought to his answer, and
have right.

No man to be arrested, or imprisoned contrary to the forme of
the great charter.

The philosophicall poet doth notably describe, the damnable and
damned proceedings of the judge of hell,

> *Gnosius hic Radamanthus habet durissima regna,*
> *Castigatque, auditque dolos, subigitque fateri.*[5]

and in another place,

> . . . . *leges fixit precio atque refixit.*[6]

First he punisheth, and then he heareth: and lastly, compelleth to
confesse and make and marre lawes at his pleasure; like as the
centurion in the holy history, did to S. Paul: For the text saith,
Centurio apprehendi Paulum jussit, et se catenis ligari et tunc in-
terrogabat, quis fuisset, et quid fecisset:[7] but good judges and
justices abhorre these courses.

Now it may be demanded, if a man be taken, or committed to
prison *contra legem terrae,*[8] against the law of the land, what remedy

4. "According to the law and custom of England."
5. "Here Cretan Radamanthus has his harshest dominions, and chastises
and examines wrongs and compels confession." Virgil, *Aeneid* vi. 566–7.
6. "He fashioned and refashioned laws at pleasure." Ibid. 622.
7. Acts 21:33, from the Vulgate. In the King James version it reads:
"Then the chief captain . . . took him and commanded him to be bound
with two chains and demanded who he was and what he had done."
8. "Against the law of the land."

hath the party grieved? To this it is answered: first, that every act of parliament made against any injury, mischiefe, or grievance doth either expressly, or impliedly give a remedy to the party wronged, or grieved: as in many of the chapters of this great charter appeareth; and therefore he may have an action grounded upon this great charter. As taking one example for many, and that in a powerfull, and a late time. Pasch. 2. H. 8. *coram rege* [9] rot. 538. against the prior of S. Oswin in Northumberland. And it is provided, and declared by the statute of 36 E. 3. that if any man feeleth himselfe grieved, contrary to any article in any statute, he shall have present remedy in chancery (that is, by originall writ) by force of the said articles and statutes.

2. He may cause him to be indicted upon this statute at the kings suite, whereof you may see a precedent Pasch. 3 H. 8. Rott. 71. *Coram rege.* Rob. Sheffields case.

3. He may have an *habeas corpus* out of the kings bench or chancery, though there be no priviledge, &c. or in the court of common pleas, or eschequer, for any officer or priviledged person there: upon which writ the gaoler must retourne, by whom he was committed, and the cause of his imprisonment, and if it appeareth that his imprisonment be just, and lawfull, he shall be remaunded to the former gaoler, but if it shall appeare to the court, that he was imprisoned against the law of the land, they ought by force of this statute to deliver him: if it be doubtfull and under consideration, he may be bailed.

In 5 E. 4. *coram rege* Rot. 143. John Keasars case, a notable record and too long here to be recited.

10 Eliz. Rot. Leas case.

In 1 & 2 Eliz. Dier. 175. Scrogs case.

In 18 Eliz. Dier. 175. Roland Hynds case *in margine.*

4. He may have an action of false imprisonment, 10 H. 7. fol. 17, but it is entred in the court of common pleas Mich. 11 H. 7. Rot. 327. Hilarie Warners case, and it appeareth by the record, that judgement was given for the plaintife: a record worthy of observation.

5. He may have a writ of *de homine replegiando.*[1]
Vide Marlebridge, cap. 8.

9. "Before the king"—i.e. citing a judgment of the Court of King's Bench.
1. "Of replevying a man." To deliver a man from custody.

6. He might by the common-law have had a writ *de odio, et atia,*[2] as you may see before, cap. 26. but that was taken away by statute, but now is revived againe by the statute of 42 E. 3. cap. 1. as there it also appeareth. It is said in W. 2. *Sed ne hujusmodi appellati, vel indictati diu detinentur in prisona, habeat breve de odio et atia, sicut in Magna Charta, et aliis statutis dict' est:* [3] and by the said act of 42 E. 3. all statutes made against Magna Charta are repealed.

(9) *Nulli vendemus* &c.) [4] This is spoken in the person of the king, who in judgement of law, in all his courts of justice is present, and repeating these words, *nulli vendemus,* &c.

And therefore, every subject of this realme, for injury done to him in *bonis, terris, vel persona,*[5] by any other subject, be he ecclesiastical or temporall, free, or bond, man, or woman, old, or young, or be he outlawed, excommunicated, or any other without exception, may take his remedy by the course of the law, and have justice, and right for the injury done to him, freely without sale, fully without any deniall, and speedily without delay.

Hereby it appeareth, that justice must have three qualities, it must be *libera, quia nihil iniquius venali justitia; plena, quia justitia non debet claudicare; et celeris, quia dilatio est quaedam negatio;* [6] and then it is both justice and right.

(10) *Nulli negabimus, aut differemus,* &c.) [7] These words have beene excellently expounded by latter acts of parliament, that by no meanes common right, or common law should be disturbed, or delayed, no, though it be commanded under the great seale, or privie seale, order, writ, letters, message or commandement whatsoever, either from the king, or any other, and that the justices shall proceede, as if no such writs, letters, order, message, or other commandement were come to them. *Judicium redditum per defaltum affirmatur, non obstante breve regis de prorogatione judicii.*[8]

That the common lawes of the realme should by no meanes be

2. "Of hatred and ill will."

3. "But lest those so prosecuted or indicted be long detained in prison, there is a writ of hatred and ill will, as said in Magna Charta and other statutes."

4. "We will sell to no one."

5. "Goods, lands, or person."

6. "Free because nothing is more unjust than venal justice; full because justice ought not to be incomplete; swift because delay is a sort of denial."

7. "To no one will we deny or delay."

8. "Judgment rendered by default is affirmed notwithstanding a writ of the king for proroguing the judgment."

delayed, for the law is the surest sanctuary, that a man can take, and the strongest fortresse to protect the weakest of all; *lex est tutissima cassis,*[9] and *sub clypeo legis nemo decipitur:*[1] but the king may stay his owne suite, as a *capias pro fine,*[2] for the king may respite his fine and the like.

All protections that are not legall, which appeare not in the Register, nor warranted by our books, are expressly against this branch, *nulli differemus:*[3] as a protection under the great seale granted to any man, directed to the sherifes, &c. and commanding them, that they shall not arrest him, during a certaine time at any other mans suite, which hath words in it, *per praerogativam nostram, quam nolumus esse arguendam;*[4] yet such protections have beene argued by the judges, according to their oath and duty, and adjudged to be void: as Mich. 11 H. 7. Rot. 124. a protection graunted to Holmes a vintner of London, his factors, servants and deputies, &c. resolved to be against law, Pasch. 7. H. 8. Rot. 66. such a protection disallowed, and the sherife amerced for not executing the writ. Mich. 13 & 14 Eliz. in Hitchcocks case, and many other of latter time: and there is a notable record of auncient time in 22 E. 1. John de Mershalls case, *non pertinet ad vicecomitem de protectione regis judicare, imo ad curiam.*[5]

(11) *Justitiam vel rectum.*)[6] Wee shall not sell, deny, or delay justice and right. *Justitiam vel rectum,* neither the end, which is justice, nor the meane, whereby we may attaine to the end, and that is the law.

Rectum, right, is taken here for law, in the same sense that *jus,*[7] often is so called. 1. Because it is the right line, whereby justice distributative is guided, and directed, and therefore all the commissions of oier, and terminer, of goale delivery, of the peace, &c. have this clause, *facturi quod ad justitiam pertinet, secundum legem,* and *consuetudinem Angliae,*[8] that is, to doe justice and right, ac-

9. "Law is the safest helmet."
1. "Under the shield of the law no one is cheated."
2. "Arrest for nonpayment of a fine."
3. "We will delay to no one."
4. "By our prerogative, which we are not willing shall be argued."
5. "It is not for the sheriff to judge but for the court."
6. "Justice or right."
7. Law as distinguished from *lex,* which is strictly *a law.*
8. "To do what pertains to justice according to the law and custom of England."

cording to the rule of the law and custome of England; and that which is called common right in 2 E. 3. is called common law, in 14 E. 3. &c. and in this sense it is taken, where it is said, *ita qd. stet recto in curia, i. legi in curia.*[9] 2. The law is called *rectum*, because it discovereth, that which is tort, crooked, or wrong, for as right signifieth law, so tort, crooked or wrong, signifieth injurie, and *injuria est contra jus*,[1] against right: *recta linea est index sui, et obliqui*,[2] hereby the crooked cord of that, which is called discretion, appeareth to be unlawfull, unlesse you take it, as it ought to be, *discretio est discernere per legem, quid sit justum.*[3] 3. It is called right, because it is the best birthright the subject hath, for thereby his goods, lands, wife, children, his body, life, honor, and estimation are protected from injury, and wrong: *major haereditas venit unicuiq; nostrum a jure, et legibus, quam a parentibus.*[4]

On chap. 30. King H. 4. graunted the measuring of woollen cloth, and canvas, that should be brought to London, to be sold by any stranger or denizen (except he were free of London) taking an ob. of every whole peece of cloth so measured of the seller, and one other ob. of the buyer, and so after that rate for a greater or lesser quantity, and one penny for the measuring of an C. ells of canvas of the seller, and so much more of the buyer; and though it were averred that two other had enjoyed the same office before with the like fees, viz. one Shearing by the same kings graunt, and one Clithew before by the graunt of R. 2. (and the truth was, Robert Pooley in 5 E. 3. and John Mareis, in 25 E. 3. had likewise enjoyed the same) yet amongst other reasons of the said judgement, it was set downe, and adjudged that the former possession was by extortion, cohertion, and without right, and that the said letters patents were in *onerationem, oppressionem, et depauperationem subditorum domini regis, &c.*[5] *et non in emendationem, ejusdem populi;*[6] and therefore the said letters patents were voyd.

9. "So that it stand to right in court, that is, the law in court."
1. "Wrong is contrary to right and law" (*jus* means both).
2. "A straight line is the indicator thereof and of what is oblique."
3. "Discretion is to discover through the law what is just."
4. "A greater inheritance comes to each of us from right and laws than from parents."
5. "In burden, oppression, and impoverishing of the subjects of the lord king."
6. "And not in emendation of his people."

3. A judgement was given in the exchequer, for an imposition set upon currants, but the common opinion was, that that judgement was against law, and divers expresse acts of parliament; and so by that which hath been said, it doth manifestly appeare.

To conclude this point, with two of the *maximes* of the common law. 1. *Le common ley ad tielment admeasure les prerogatives le roy, que ilz no tolleront, ne prejudiceront le inheritance dascun,*[7] the common law hath so admeasured the prerogatives of the king, that they should not take away, nor prejudice the inheritance of any: and the best inheritance that the subject hath, is the law of the realme. 2. *Nihil tam proprium est imperii, quam legibus vivere.*[8]

Upon this chapter, as by the said particulars may appeare, this conclusion is necessarily gathered, that all monopolies concerning trade and traffique, are against the liberty and freedome, declared and graunted by this great charter, and against divers other acts of parliament, which are good commentaries upon this chapter.

Case of Prohibitions del roy, 1612 (conference between King James I and the Judges of England. 12 Coke, 63. Coke, who was chief justice and spokesman of the judges, is reporting this).

Note: Upon Sunday, the 10th of November of this same term, the king, upon complaint made to him by Bancroft, Archbishop of Canterbury, concerning prohibitions, was informed that when the question was made of what matters the ecclesiastical Judges have cognizance, either upon the opposition of the statute concerning tithes, or any other thing ecclesiastical, or upon the statute i El. concerning the high commission, or in any other case in which there is not express authority in law, the King himself may decide it in his royal person; and that the Judges are but the delegates of the king, and that the king may take what causes he shall please to determine from the determination of the Judges, and may determine them himself. And the Archbishop said that this was clear in divinity that such authority belongs to the king by the word of God in the scripture. To which it was answered by me in the presence and with the clear consent of all the Judges of England, and Barons of the

7. Law French: "The common law has so admeasured the prerogatives of the king that they do not take away or prejudice the inheritance of anyone."

8. "Nothing is so properly characteristic of government as living by laws."

Exchequer, that the King in his own person cannot adjudge any case, either criminal as treason, felony, &c. or betwixt party and party concerning his inheritance, chattels or goods, &c., but this ought to be determined and adjudged in some court of justice, according to the law and custom of England, and always judgments are given, *ideo consideratum est per curiam* [9] so that the court gives the judgment; and the King hath his court viz: in the upper house of Parliament, in which he with his lords is the supreme Judge over all other judges; for if error be in the Common Pleas, that may be reversed in the King's Bench; and if the court of King's Bench err, that may be reversed in the upper house of Parliament, by the King with the assent of the Lords spiritual and temporal, without the Commons, in this respect the King is called Chief Justice, and it appears in our books that the King may sit in the Star Chamber, but this was to consult with the Justices upon certain questions proposed to them, and not *in judicio;* [1] so in the King's Bench he may sit, but the court gives the judgment; and it is commonly said in our books that the king is always present in the court in judgment of law, but upon this he cannot be nonsuit; but the judgments are always given *per curiam;* [2] and the Judges are sworn to execute justice according to law and the custom of England. And it appears by the Act of Parliament of 2 Ed. 3 cap. 9, 2 Ed. 3, cap. 1, that neither by the great seal nor by the little seal justice shall be delayed; *ergo,* [3] the king cannot take any cause out of any of his Courts, and give judgment upon it himself, but in his own cause he may stay it, it as it doth appear. 11 H. 4. 8. And the judges informed the King that no King after the Conquest assumed to himself to give any judgment in any cause whatever, which concerned the administration of justice, within this realm, but these were solely determined by the courts of justice: and the king cannot arrest any man, as the book is in 1 H. 7. 4. for the party cannot have remedy against the King: so if the King give any judgment what remedy can the party have? Vide 39 Ed. 3 one who had a judgment reversed before the council of state; it was held utterly void, for that it was not a place where judgment may be reversed. Vide 1 H. 7. 4. Hussey, Chief

9. "It is therefore considered by the court."
1. "In the course of judicial decision."
2. "By the court."
3. "Therefore."

Justice, who was Attorney to Ed. 4 reports that Sir John Markham, Chief Justice, said to King Edw. 4 that the King cannot arrest a man for suspicion of treason or felony, as others of his lieges may; for that if it be wrong to the party grieved, he can have no remedy; and it was greatly marvelled that the Archbishop durst inform the King that such absolute power and authority as is aforesaid belonged to the King by Word of God. Vide 4 H. 4 Cap. 22, which being translated into Latin, the effect is, *judicia in curia Regis reddita non annihiletur, sed stet judicium in suo robore quosque per judicium curiae Regis tanquam erroneum,*[4] &c. Vide West 2 cap. 5. Vide le stat, de Marlbridge, Cap. 1. *Provisum est concordatum, et concessum, quod tam majores quam minores iustitiam habeant et recipiant in curia domini Regis, et vide le stat. de Magna Carta,*[5] cap. 29, 25 Ed. 3. cap. 5. None may be taken by petition or suggestion made to our lord the King or his council, unless by judgment: and 43 Ed. 3. cap. 3, no man shall be put to answer without presentment before the Justices, matter of record, or by due proofs, or by writ original according to the ancient law of the land: and if anything be done against it, it shall be void in law and held for error. Vide 28 Ed. 3 c. 3. 37 Ed. 3. cap. 18. Vide 17 R. 2. *ex rotulis Parliamenti in Turri,*[6] art. 10. A controversy of land between parties was heard by the king, and sentence given, which was repealed, for this, that it did belong to the common law. Then the King said that he thought the law was founded upon reason, and that he and others had reason as well as the judges: to which it was answered by me that true it was, that God had endowed his Majesty with excellent science, and great endowments of nature; but his Majesty was not learned in the laws of his realm of England, and causes which concern the life, or inheritance, or goods or fortunes of his subjects, are not to be decided by natural reason, but by the artificial reason and judgment of law, which law is an art which requires long study and experience before that a man can attain to the cognizance of it; and that the law was the golden met wand and measure to try the causes of the subjects

4. "Judgments in the king's courts shall not be annulled but let the judgment stand in its strength until by the judgment of the king's court, however erroneous."

5. "It is provided, agreed, and granted that both the greater and the lesser have and receive justice in the court of the lord king, and see the statute of Magna Carta."

6. "From the rolls of Parliament in the Tower."

and which protected his Majesty in safety and peace; with which the King was greatly offended and said that then he should be under the law, which was treason to affirm, as he said: to which I said that Bracton saith, *quod Rex non debet esse sub homine, sed sub Deo et lege*.[7]

The Petition of Right, 1627 (7 Pickering, *Statutes at Large*, 317–20).

The petition exhibited to his Majesty by the lords spiritual and temporal, and commons, in this present parliament assembled, concerning divers rights and liberties of the subjects, with the King's majesty's royal answer thereunto in full parliament.

To the King's most excellent majesty.

Humbly shew unto our sovereign lord the King, the lords spiritual and temporal, and commons in parliament assembled, That whereas it is declared and enacted by a statute made in the time of the reign of King Edward the First commonly called Statutum de tallagio non concedendo, That no tallage or aid shall be laid or levied by the King or his heirs in this realm, without the good will and assent of the archbishops, bishops, earls, barons, knights, burgesses, and other freemen of the commonalty of this realm; (2) and by authority of parliament holden in the five and twentieth year of the reign of King Edward the Third, it is declared and enacted, That from thenceforth no person should be compelled to make any loans to the King against his will, because such loans were against reason and the franchise of the land; (3) and by other laws of this realm it is provided, That none should be charged by any charge or imposition called a benevolence, nor by such like charge: (4) by which the statutes before mentioned, and other the good laws and statutes of this realm, your subjects have inherited this freedom, That they should not be compelled to contribute to any tax, tallage, aid or other like charge not set by common consent in Parliament.

II. Yet nevertheless, of late divers commissions directed to sundry commissioners in several countries, with instructions, have issued; by means whereof your people have been in divers places assembled, and required to lend certain sums of money unto your Majesty, and many of them, upon their refusal so to do, have had an oath

7. "That the king ought not to be under man, but under God and the law."

administered unto them not warrantable by the laws or statutes of this realm, and have been constrained to become bound to make appearance and give attendance before your privy council and in other places, and others of them have been therefore imprisoned, confined, and sundry other ways molested and disquieted; (2) and divers other charges have been laid and levied upon your people in several counties by lord lieutenants, deputy lieutenants, commissioners for musters, justices of peace and others, by command or direction from your Majesty, or your privy council, against the laws and free customs of the realm.

III. And where also by the statute called The great charter of the liberties of England, it is declared and enacted, That no freeman may be taken or imprisoned, or be disseised of his freehold or liberties, or his free customs, or be outlawed or exiled, or in manner destroyed, but by the lawful judgment of his peers, or by the law of the land.

IV. And in the eight and twentieth year of the reign of King Edward the Third, it was declared and enacted by authority of parliament, That no man of what estate or condition that he be, should be put out of his land or tenements, nor taken nor imprisoned, nor disherited, nor put to death without being brought to answer by due process of law:

V. Nevertheless against the tenor of the said statutes, and other the good laws and statutes of your realm to that end provided, divers of your subjects have of late been imprisoned without any cause shewed; (2) and when for their deliverance they were brought before your justices by your Majesty's writs of habeas corpus, there to undergo and receive as the court should order, and their keepers commanded to certify the causes of their detainer, no cause was certified, but that they were detained by your Majesty's special command, signified by the lords of your privy council, and yet were returned back to several prisons, without being charged with any thing to which they might make answer according to the law:

VI. And whereas of late great companies of soldiers and mariners have been dispersed into divers counties of the realm, and the inhabitants against their wills have been compelled to receive them into their houses, and there to suffer them to sojourn, against the laws and customs of this realm, and to the great grievance and vexation of the people:

VII. And whereas also by authority of parliament, in the five and twentieth year of the reign of King Edward the Third, it is declared and enacted, That no man should be forejudged of life or limb against the form of the great charter and the law of the land; (2) and by the said great charter and other the laws and statutes of this your realm, no man ought to be adjudged to death but by the laws established in this your realm, either by the customs of the same realm, or by acts of parliament: (3) and whereas no offender of what kind soever is exempt from the proceedings to be used, and punishments to be inflicted by the laws and statutes of this your realm: nevertheless of late time divers commissions under your Majesty's great seal have issued forth, by which certain persons have been assigned and appointed commissioners with power and authority to proceed within the land, according to the justice of martial law, against such soldiers or mariners, or other dissolute persons joining with them, as should commit any murder, robbery, felony, mutiny or other outrage or misdemeanor whatsoever, and by such summary course and order as is agreeable to martial law, and as is used in armies in time of war, to proceed to the trial and condemnation of such offenders, and them to cause to be executed and put to death according to the law martial:

VIII. By pretext whereof some of your Majesty's subjects have been by some of the said commissioners put to death, when and where, if by the laws and statutes of the land they had deserved death, by the same laws and statutes also they might, and by no other ought to have been judged and executed:

IX. And also sundry grievous offenders, by colour thereof claiming an exemption, have escaped the punishments due to them by the laws and statutes of this your realm, by reason that divers of your officers and ministers of justice have unjustly refused or forborn to proceed against such offenders according to the same laws and statutes, upon pretence that the said offenders were punishable only by martial law, and by authority of such commissions as aforesaid: (2) which commissions, and all other of like nature, are wholly and directly contrary to the said laws and statutes of this your realm:

X. They do therefore humbly pray your most excellent Majesty, That no man hereafter be compelled to make or yield any gift, loan, benevolence, tax, or such like charge, without common consent by act of parliament; (2) and that none be called to make answer, or take such oath, or to give attendance, or be confined, or otherwise molested or disquieted concerning the same, or for refusal thereof; (3) and that no freeman, in any such manner as is before-mentioned, be imprisoned or detained; (4) and that your Majesty would be pleased to remove the said soldiers and mariners, and that your people may not be so burthened in time to come; (5) and that the aforesaid commissions, for proceeding by martial law, may be revoked and annulled; and that hereafter no commissions of like nature may issue forth to any person or persons whatsoever to be executed as aforesaid, lest by colour of them any of your Majesty's subjects be destroyed, or put to death contrary to the laws and franchise of the land.

XI. All which they most humbly pray of your most excellent Majesty as their rights and liberties, according to the laws and statutes of this realm; and that your Majesty would also vouchsafe to declare, That the awards, doings and proceedings, to the prejudice of your people in any of the premisses, shall not be drawn hereafter into consequence or example; (2) and that your Majesty would be also graciously pleased, for the further comfort and safety of your people, to declare your royal will and pleasure, That in the things aforesaid all your officers and ministers shall serve you according to the laws and statutes of this realm, as they tender the honour of your Majesty, and the prosperity of this kingdom. *Qua quidem petitione lecta & plenius intellecta per dictum dominum regem taliter est responsum in pleno parliamento, viz. Soit droit fait come est desire.*[8]

Lord Cromwell's Case, King's Bench, 1578 (4 Coke, 12b).

Henry Lord Cromwell brought an action *de scandalis magnatum* [9] against Edward Denny, vicar of Northlinham in the county of Norfolk, *tam pro dom' Regina, quam pro seipso;* [1] and declared upon the stat. of 2 R. 2 cap. 5. that if any contrive *aliqua falsa nova, horribilia et falsa nuncia de praelatis, ducibus, comitibus, et aliis proceribus et magnatibus, regni,*[2] &c. by which debate may arise

8. "Which petition, indeed, having been read and fully understood by the said lord king was answered in full Parliament, namely: Let right be done as is desired."
9. "For slander of great men.
1. "Both for our lady the queen and for himself."
2. "Any false news, horrible and false messages, about prelates, dukes, earls, and other noblemen and great men of the kingdom."

betwixt the Lords and Commons (which God forbid) by which danger, mischief and destruction may happen to the whole realm, &c. and *quicunque contra fecerit*,[3] shall incur the penalty of the stat. of W. I. c. 33. And the defendant was charged that he said to the plaintiff, then a baron of the realm, "It is no marvel that you like not of me, for you like of those that maintain sedition against the Queen's proceedings." The defendant justified the words, upon which the plaintiff demurred, and the bar was held insufficient. And Term' Trin' anno 23 Eliz. in arrest of judgment it was moved by the defendant's counsel, that the declaration was insufficient, because the said act of 2 R. 2. was misrecited; for the words of the act are, *Si ascun controver ascun faux nouvelles et horribles et faux messoinges*,[4] which word *"messoinges"* he who translated the statutes at large into English, has translated "messages" which was the reason that he who drew the declaration in the case at bar inserted the said word "nuncia" where it should be *mendacia*.[5] 2. The said act saith, "and whosoever shall do it, shall incur, &c." And the plaintiff in his declaration saith, *et quicunq; contra fecerit*,[6] which is as much as to say, "who shall not do it;" but against that·it was objected, that the said act was a private act, it concerning only the prelates, nobles, and certain great officers, whereof the court would not take notice ex officio; and therefore the court ought to take the act as the party has alleged it: but it was resolved by Wray, Chief Justice, Sir Thomas Gawdy, *et totam curiam*,[7] that it was such act, whereof the court ought to take notice; and *eo magis* [8] because it by a means concerns the King himself. 1. Forasmuch as it touches the prelates, nobles, and great offices, which are of the King's council, and of eminent qualities, and serve him in so high and honourable offices, which they have under the King, and by his royal authority have the administration of justice of his subjects, by which it appears that the slandering of them principally concerns the King himself in his royal government. 2. Forasmuch as the statute saith, that danger, mischief, and destruction may happen to the whole realm, &c. that

3. "Whoever shall act to the contrary."
4. "If anyone contrives any false news and horrible and false messages."
5. "Lies."
6. "And whoever shall act contrary."
7. "And the whole court."
8. "The more."

also concerns the King, for he is the head of the realm; and these are the reasons that always such actions de scandalis magnatum have been brought upon the said statute *tam pro domino rege quam pro seipso*,[9] and of all statutes which concern the King, the judges ought to take notice. It was likewise resolved that if the act was private, and that the court ought to take it to be such as is alleged; then the said act was against law and reason, and therefore void: for as it is alleged, those who do not offend shall be punished, and that was *condemnare insontem et demittere reum;*[1] wherefore judgment was given against the plaintiff *quod nihil capiat per billam.*[2]

Dr. Bonham's Case, Common Pleas, 1610 (8 Coke, 114).

[Action of trespass for false imprisonment by Dr. Bonham against the censors or governors of the Royal College of Physicians, a corporation chartered by Henry VIII, the charter of which was confirmed by an act of Parliament of Queen Mary. The statute provided:

> That whensoever the president of the college, or commonalty of the faculty of physic at London for the time being, or such as the said president and college shall yearly, according to the tenor and meaning of the said act, authorize to search, examine, correct, and punish all offenders and transgressors in the said faculty, &c. shall send or commit any such offender or offenders for his or their offence or disobedience, contrary to any article or clause contained in the said grant or act, to any ward, gaol, or prison within the same city (the Tower of London except) that then from time to time the warden, gaoler, or keeper, &c. shall receive, &c. such person so offending, &c. and the same shall keep at his proper charge, without bail or mainprize, until such time as such offender or disobedient be discharged of the said imprisonment by the said president, and such persons as shall be thereunto authorised, upon pain that all and every such warden, gaoler, &c. doing the contrary, shall lose and forfeit the double of such fines and amerciaments as such offender and offenders shall be assessed to pay, by such as the said president and college shall authorise as aforesaid, so that the fine and amerciament be not at any one time above the sum of 20£. the

9. "As well for the lord king as for himself."
1. "Condemn the innocent and dismiss the guilty."
2. "That he take nothing by his bill."

one moiety to the King, the other moiety to the president and college, &c.

Bonham under the terms of the charter confirmed by the statute was fined £10 by the censors and imprisoned for nonpayment and contempt of the authority of the censors. By the charter the fine was payable half to the crown and half to the college. After full statement of the facts, the report reads]:

As to the two points upon which the Chief Justice, Warburton and Daniel, gave judgment: 1. It was resolved by them, that the said censors had not power to commit the plaintiff for any of the causes mentioned in the bar; and the cause and reason thereof shortly was, that the said clause, which gives power to the said censors to fine and imprison, doth not extend to the said clause, *sc. quod nemo in dicta civitate &c. exerceat dictam facultatem &c.*[3] which prohibits every one from practising physic in London, &c. without licence from the president and college; but extends only to punish those who practise physic in London, *pro delictis suis in non bene exequendo, faciendo & utendo facultatem medicinae,*[4] by fine and imprisonment: so that the censors have not power by the letters patent, and the act, to fine or imprison any for practising physic in London, but only *pro delictis suis in non bene exequendo, &c. sc.*[5] for ill, and not good use and practice of physic. And that was made manifest by five reasons, which were called *vividae rationes,*[6] because they had their vigour and life from the letters patent, and the act itself; and the best expositor of all letters patent, and acts of Parliament, are the letters patent and the acts of Parliament themselves, by construction, and conferring all the parts of them together, (a) *Optima statuti interpretatrix est (omnibus particulis ejusdem inspectis) ipsum statutum;*[7] and (b) *injustum est nisi tota lege inspecta una aliqua ejus particula proposita judicare vel respondere.*[8]

3. "That no one in said city, etc. should pursue the said profession."
4. "For his offenses in not well pursuing, carrying on, and using the practice of medicine."
5. "For his offenses in not well pursuing."
6. "Vivid reasons."
7. "The statute itself, all its particulars having been looked into, is the best interpreter of a statute."
8. Unless the whole law has been looked into it is unjust to judge or give an opinion on a particular proposition."

4. The censors cannot be judges, ministers, and parties; judges to give sentence or judgment; ministers to make summons; and parties to have the moiety of the forfeiture, *quia aliquis non debet esse Judex in propria causa, imo iniquum est aliquem suae rei esse judicem;* [9] and one cannot be Judge and attorney for any of the parties, Dyer 3 E. 6. 65. 38. E. 3. 15. 8 H. 6. 19. b. 20. a. 21 E. 4. 47. a. &c. And it appears in our books that in many cases, the common law will controul acts of Parliament, and sometimes adjudge them to be utterly void: for when an act of Parliament is against common right and reason, or repugnant, or impossible to be performed, the common law will controul it, and adjudge such act to be void; and therefore in 8 E. 3. 30. a. b. Thomas Tregor's case on the statute of W. 2. c. 38. & *artic' super chartas*,[1] c. 9. Herle saith, some statutes are made against law and right, which those who made them perceiving, would not put them in execution: the stat: of W. 2. c. 21 gives a writ of *Cessavit* [2] *haeredi petenti super haeredem tenent' & super eos quibus alienatum fuerit hujusmodi tenementum:* [3] and yet it is adjudged in 33 E. 3. Cessavit 42. where the case was, two coparceners lords, and tenant by fealty and certain rent, one coparcener had issu and died, the aunt and the niece shall not join in a *Cessavit,* because the heir shall not have a *Cessavit* for the cesser in the time of his ancestor, F. N. B. 209. F. and therewith agrees Plow. Com. 110. a. and the reason is, because in a *Cessavit* the tenant before judgment may render the arrearages and damages, &c. and retain his land, and that he cannot do when the heir brings a *Cessavit,* for the cesser in the time of his ancestor, for the arrearages incurred in the life of the ancestor do not belong to the heir: and because it would be against common right and reason, the common law adjudges the said act of Parliament as to that point void. The statute of Carlisle, made anno 35 E.I. enacts, that the order of the Cistercians and Augustines, who have a convent and common seal, that the common seal shall be in the keeping of the Prior, who is under the Abbot, and four others of the most grave of the house, and that any deed sealed

9. Because one ought not to be judge in his own case; indeed it is unjust for anyone to be judge of his own affair."

1. "Articles additional to the charters."

2. Writ of Cessavit—an action where the tenant has ceased to pay rent or render service for two years.

3. [Cessavit] "The heir suing the heir of the tenant and those to whom a tenement of this sort has been alienated."

with the common seal, which is not so in keeping shall be void: and the opinion of the court (in an. 27 H. 6. Annuity 41.) was, that this statute was void, for it is impertinent to be observed, for the seal being in their keeping, the Abbot cannot seal anything with it, and when it is in the Abbot's hands, it is out of their keeping *ipso facto;* [4] and if the statute should be observed, every common seal shall be defeated upon a simple surmise, which cannot be tried. Note reader the words of the said statute of Carlisle, *anno* 35 E. 1. (which is called *Statutum religiosorum*) [5] are, *Et insuper ordinavit dominus Rex & statuit, quod Abbates Cisterc' & Praemonstraten' ordin' religiosorum, &c. de caetero habeant sigillum commune, et illud in custodia Prioris monasterii seu domus, et quatuor de dignioribus et discretioribus ejusdem loci conventus sub privato sigillo Abbatis ipsius loci custod' depo', &c. Et si forsan aliqua scripta obligationum, donationum, emptionum, venditionum, alienationum, seu aliorum quorumcunque, contractuum alio sigillo quam tali sigillo communi sicut praemittit' custodit' inveniant' a modo sigillat', pro nullo penitus habeantur omnique careant firmitate.* [6] So the statute of 1 E. 6. c. 14. gives chauntries, &c. to the King, saving to the donor, &c. all such rents, services, &c. and the common law controuls it, and adjudges it void as to services, and the donor shall have the rent, as a rentseck, distrainable of common right, for it would be against common right and reason that the King should hold of any, or do service to any of his subjects, 14 Eliz. Dyer 313. and so it was adjudged Mich. 16 & 17 Eliz. in Com' Banco in Strowd's case. So if any act of Parliament gives to any to hold, or to have conusans of all manner of pleas arising before him within his manor of D. yet he shall hold no plea, to which he himself is party; for, as hath been said, *iniquum est aliquem suae rei esse judicem.* [7]

4. "By that very fact."

5. "Statute of the religious" (i.e. with respect to monks).

6. "And further the lord king ordains that Abbots of Cistercian and Praemonstratensian orders of monks, etc. for the rest have a common seal and deposit it in the custody of the prior of the monastery or house and of four of the more worthy and discreet of the assembly of that place under the private seal of the abbot of that place, and if by chance any writing of obligations, gifts, buyings, sellings, alienations, or any other contracts under another seal than such common seal as aforesaid in custody appear in sealed form they shall be held wholly for nought and lack all validity."

7. "It is unjust for anyone to be judge of his own affair."

Day v. Savadge, Common Pleas, 1615 (Hobart, 85. The case is reported by Sir Henry Hobart, who was Lord Chief Justice).

Matthew Day brought an action of trespass against John Savadge for taking away a bag of nutmegs. The defendant pleaded that the city of London is an ancient city, and so had been time out of mind, and that the mayor, citizens and commonalty had been all that time a corporate body, and seised of a bank or wharf in London, called Queenhithe, and by all that time have used to have and take for goods laid upon the same wharf, to be conveyed from thence by water, of persons not lawfully thereof discharged, wharfage, that is to say, a halfpenny for every porter's burthen there laid to be so conveyed; and for default of payment, to distres such goods upon the said wharf, by a person by the mayor to be appointed for the collection; and then shows, that two persons unknown brought two porters' burthens of the goods of the said plaintiff, being no person lawfully discharged, whereof the bag of nutmegs in question was part, and laid them upon the said wharf to be conveyed by water; and that the defendant, being appointed collector, &c. demands two halfpence, and because they were not paid, distrained, &c. as was lawful for him to do. The plaintiff, by way of replication, confessed all the bar in general, and laid, that within the said city there was, and time out of mind had been, a custom, that all the freemen of the said city, had been, and ought to be discharged of the said payment of wharfage of their goods, and averred that he was a freeman of the said city, &c. The said defendant said, that there was no such custom within the said city, *et hoc paratus est verificare ubi et quando et prout curia consideravit;* [8] and then adds a surmise thus; *super quo praed. John. Savadge dicit quod in civitate praed.* [9] there is, and time out of mind hath been, a custom, that when any issue &c. upon any custom of the said city is joined, though the mayor, commonalty and citizens be parties to the action, the mayor and aldermen of the city have used to certify to the justices the truth of such custom; and that the said custom and all other customs of the said city, by authority of parliament, in the seventh year of Richard the second, was confirmed; and prayed the king's writ to the mayor and aldermen of the said city to

8. "And this he is ready to verify where and when and as the court shall have considered."

9. "Upon which the said John Savadge says that in said City."

certify, &c. And the said plaintiff saith, that the said issue ought to be tried by jury, and not by certificate, and that such custom alleged by the defendant for the trial by certificate *ut supra,* is against the law and common reason, and prayeth judgment, and that the cause may be tried by jury; whereupon the defendant demurreth.

After some arguments at the bar *pro et contra,* wherein nothing was questioned but whether the custom in this special case were good, that the mayor and aldermen should certify a custom which concerned the interest of the corporation whereof they were a part, the court now being agreed determined to give judgment, and intreated me to pronounce it for them all; and so we gave judgment, that this custom was not to be tried by certificate, but by the jury; whereof I gave three reasons.

The first, that it was not properly a custom, but a kind of prescription, or in the nature of a prescription, and then clearly it was not within their custom.

Secondly, that it was no such custom as was within the reason or meaning of that special peculiar form of trial by certificate, that was granted and used in London.

Thirdly, it was against right and justice, and against natural equity to allow them their certificate, wherein they are to try and judge their own cause. . . .

By that which hath been said it appears, that though in pleading it were confessed, that the custom of certificate of the customs of London is confirmed by parliament, yet it made no change in this case, both because it is none of the customs intended, and because even an act of parliament, made against natural equity, as to make a man judge in his own case, is void in itself; for *jura naturae sunt immutabilia,*[1] and they are *leges legum.*[2]

Holt, C. J., in King v. Earl of Banbury, King's Bench, 1695 (Skinner, 517, 526–7).

Every Law which binds the subjects of this Realm, ought to be either the Common Law and Usage of the Realm, or Act of Parliament, Nec super eum ibimus, nec super eum mittemus nisi per legale judicium parium suorum, aut per legem terrae; and there-

---

1. "The laws of nature are immutable."
2. "The laws of laws."

fore the Earl of Banbury cannot be ousted of his Dignity but by Attainder, or Act of Parliament, or Judgment in a Scire facias upon his Patent; but if there was any such Law and Custom of Parliament, (the which Mr. Attorney said was inter arcana imperii, which is a strange notion of a Law, though it may be good in politicks; and for which the Lords would not thank him, when they considered that the Law which governs the Inheritance of their Dignities is inter arcana, for misera est servitus ubi jus est vagum & incertum,) yet when this comes incidently in Question before them, they ought to adjudge and intermeddle with it, and they adjudge Things of as high a Nature every Day; for they construe and expound Acts of Parliament, and adjudge them to be void; they discharge men committed by Parliament upon a prorogation, they adjudge of privilege of Parliament, and instanced in the Case of Sir George Binion, and Sir John Evelin in C. B. where the question was, if the filing of an original during a session, against a member, be a breach of privilege; and adjudged no breach; and he said that they did but march in the steps of their predecessors, who have adjudged and determined of matters of as high a nature as this; and he cited the case out of an Oxford manuscript, where upon a counterplea of voucher, the court of C. B. was divided in opinion; and upon this there was an Order by the Lords, that they should adjudge the counterplea good; but when this order came into C. B. Parning Chief Justice refused to give judgment, but Chard in his absence took an opportunity, and gave judgment, upon which a Writ of Error was brought, and all this matter shewn in R. B. and that there was an Order by the Lords, &c. but the court did not regard it, but reversed the judgment; and he said, that the Journal of the Lords, is not any Record, but notes and memorials for the Clerks to perfect and enter the Records, and cited Hobart; and so the judgment which they have shewn in their Replication, is not any judgment or determination in Parliament; and if it was, yet it is in an original cause of which they have not conusance, and of a matter which was not submitted, or before them for their determination, and they have not given any judgment, by which he shall be barred or excluded from his Peerage; and he having made a good title in his plea, the which is not answered or avoided by the Replication, it appears that he is a Peer, and ought to be indicted by his proper name, scil. Charles, Earl of Banbury;

and being indicted by the name of Charles Knollys, Esq; this is a Misnomer, for which the indictment ought to be abated; and therefore he ruled, that it be abated.

City of London v. Wood, Before Commissioners, on Error, 1701 (12 Modern, 669).

[Action of debt in the Mayor's Court of the City of London to recover for a forfeiture to the city under a bylaw of the city. On judgment against the defendant, error was brought. Four points were raised, of which the fourth was "whether this action be brought in a proper court, it being for a forfeiture to the city."]

Hatsell, B. But another error assigned is that this action is brought by the Mayor and commonalty of London in a court holden before the Mayor and alderman; and the record says that the Mayor and commonalty of London came before that court, that is, the Mayor and commonalty came before the Mayor and aldermen; so that the Mayor is both judge and party, a thing against natural justice . . . And he quoted Hob. 87 that an act of Parliament against natural equity, as to make one a judge in his own cause would be merely void.

Holt, C. J. . . . But the true great point is, that the court is held before the Mayor and aldermen, and the action brought in the names of the Mayor and commonalty; and that very man, who is head of the city, and without whom the city has no ability or capacity to sue, is the very person before whom the action is brought; and this cannot be by the rules of any law whatever, for it is against all laws that the same person should be party and judge in the same cause, for it is manifest contradiction; for the party is he that is to complain to the judge, and the judge is to hear the party; the party endeavors to have his will, the judge determines against the will of the party, and has authority to enforce him to obey his sentence; and can any man act against his own will, or enforce himself to obey? The judge is agent, the party is patient, and the same person cannot be both agent and patient in the same thing; but it is the same thing to say that the same man may be patient and agent in the same thing, as to say that he may be judge and party; and it is manifest contradiction. And what my Lord Coke says in Dr. Bonham's Case in his 8 Co. is far from any extravagancy, for it is a very reasonable and true saying, That if an act of parliament should ordain that the same person should be party and judge, or, which is the same thing, judge in his own cause, it would be a void act of parliament; for it is impossible that one should be judge and party, for the judge is to determine between party and party, or between the government and the party; and an act of parliament can do no wrong, though it may do several things that look pretty odd; for it may discharge one from his allegiance to the government he lives under, and restore his to the state of nature; but it cannot make one that lives under a government judge and party. An act of parliament may not make adultery lawful, that is, it cannot make it lawful for A. to lie with the wife of B. but it may make the wife of A. to be the wife of B. and dissolve her marriage with A.

English Bill of Rights, 1688 (Statute I Wm. & Mary, Session 2, chap. 2).

[An act declaring the rights and liberties of the subject, and settling the succession of the crown.]

WHEREAS the lords spiritual and temporal, and commons, assembled at Westminster, lawfully, fully, and freely representing all the estates of the people of this realm, did upon the thirteenth day of February, in the year of our Lord one thousand six hundred eighty eight, present unto their Majesties, then called and known by the names and stile of William and Mary, prince and princess of Orange, being present in their proper persons, a certain declaration in writing, made by the said lords and commons, in the words following; viz.

WHEREAS the late King James the Second, by the assistance of divers evil counsellors, judges, and ministers employed by him, did endeavour to subvert and extirpate the protestant religion, and the laws and liberties of this kingdom.

1. By assuming and exercising a power of dispensing with and suspending of laws, and the execution of laws, without consent of parliament.

2. By committing and prosecuting divers worthy prelates, for humbly petitioning to be excused from concurring to the said assumed power.

3. By issuing and causing to be executed a commission under the great seal for erecting a court called, The court of commissioners for ecclesiastical causes.

4. By levying money for and to the use of the crown, by pretence of prerogative, for other time, and in other manner, than the same was granted by parliament.

5. By raising and keeping a standing army within this kingdom in time of peace, without consent of parliament, and quartering soldiers contrary to law.

6. By causing several good subjects, being protestants, to be disarmed, at the same time when papists were both armed and employed, contrary to law.

7. By violating the freedom of election of members to serve in parliament.

8. By prosecutions in the court of King's bench, for matters and causes cognizable only in parliament; and by divers other arbitrary and illegal courses.

9. And whereas of late years, partial, corrupt, and unqualified persons have been returned and served on juries in trials, and particularly divers jurors in trials for high treason, which were not freeholders.

10. And excessive bail hath been required of persons committed in criminal cases, to elude the benefit of the laws made for the liberty of the subjects.

11. And excessive fines have been imposed; and illegal and cruel punishments inflicted.

12. And several grants and promises made of fines and forfeitures, before any conviction or judgment against the persons, upon whom the same were to be levied.

All which are utterly and directly contrary to the known laws and statutes, and freedom of this realm.

And whereas the said late King James the Second having abdicated the government, and the throne being thereby vacant, his highness the prince of Orange (whom it has pleased Almighty God to make the glorious instrument of delivering this kingdom from popery and arbitrary power) did (by the advice of the lords spiritual and temporal, and divers principal persons of the commons) cause letters to be written to the lords spiritual and temporal, being protestants; and other letters to the several counties, cities, universities, boroughs, and cinque-ports, for the choosing of such persons to represent them, as were of right to be sent to parliament, to meet and sit at Westminster, upon the two and twentieth day of January, in this year one thousand six hundred eighty and eight, in order to such an establishment, as that their religion, laws, and liberties might not again be in danger of being subverted: upon which letters, elections have been accordingly made.

And thereupon the said lords spiritual and temporal, and commons, pursuant to their respective letters and elections, being now assembled in a full and free representative of this nation, taking into their most serious consideration the best means for attaining the ends aforesaid; do in the first place (as their ancestors in like case have usually done) for the vindicating and asserting their ancient rights and liberties, declare;

1. That the pretended power of suspending of laws, or the execution of laws, by regal authority, without consent of parliament, is illegal.

2. That the pretended power of dispensing with laws, or the execution of laws, by regal authority, as it hath been assumed and exercised of late, is illegal.

3. That the commission for erecting the late court of commissioners for ecclesiastical causes, and all other commissions and courts of like nature are illegal and pernicious.

4. That levying money for or to the use of the crown, by pretence of prerogative, without grant of parliament, for longer time, or in other manner than the same is or shall be granted, is illegal.

5. That it is the right of the subjects to petition the King, and all commitments and prosecutions for such petitioning are illegal.

6. That the raising or keeping a standing army within the kingdom in time of peace, unless it be with consent of parliament, is against law.

7. That the subjects which are protestants, may have arms for their defence suitable to their conditions, and as allowed by law.

8. That election of members of parliament ought to be free.

9. That the freedom of speech, and debates or proceedings in parliament, ought not to be impeached or questioned in any court or place out of parliament.

10. That excessive bail ought not to be required, nor excessive fines imposed; nor cruel and unusual punishments inflicted.

11. That jurors ought to be duly impanelled and returned, and jurors which pass upon men in trials for high treason ought to be freeholders.

12. That all grants and promises of fines and forfeitures of particular persons before conviction, are illegal and void.

13. And that for redress of all grievances, and for the amending, strengthening, and preserving of the laws, parliaments ought to be held frequently.

And they do claim, demand, and insist upon all and singular the premisses, as their undoubted rights and liberties; and that no declarations, judgments, doings or proceedings, to the prejudice of the people in any of the said premisses, ought in any wise to be drawn hereafter into consequence or example.

Provisions of Colonial Charters.

New Hampshire: commission of 1680 provides for veto by Privy Council on legislation and appeal from local courts to Privy Council.

Massachusetts: charter of 1629, "laws not contrary to laws and statutes of England"; charter of 1691, same provision.

Rhode Island: charter of 1663, "laws not repugnant to the laws of England."

Connecticut: charter of 1662, "laws not contrary to the laws of England."

New York: royal grant to the Duke of York, 1664 and 1674, "laws according to the laws of England."

New Jersey: grants to the Duke of York and to Penn, same provision.

Pennsylvania: charter of 1681, "laws not repugnant to the laws of England," appeal to Privy Council; frame of government, 1683, "no laws repugnant to the charter," the provisions of Magna Carta as to justice, guarantee of jury trial; charter of privileges, 1701, freedom of worship (art. 1), accused to be allowed witnesses and counsel (art. 5), appeals in cases involving property (art. 6).

Delaware: charter of 1701, same provisions as in Pennsylvania charter of privileges, arts. 1, 5, 6.

Maryland: charter of 1632, "statutes not to be repugnant to the laws of England."

Virginia: third charter, 1611–12, "laws not contrary to the laws of England."

North Carolina: charter of Carolina, 1663, "laws agreeable to the laws and customs of England"; charter of 1665, the same, and also freedom of worship.

South Carolina: the same.

Georgia: charter of 1732, "laws not contrary to the laws of England."

South Carolina, Act of December 12, 1712 (Grimke, *Public Laws of South Carolina,* no. 331, p. 25).

§ 3. All the Statutes of the Kingdom of England relating to the allegiance of the people, to her present Majesty Queen Anne, and her lawful successors, and the several public oaths, and subscribing the tests required of the people of England in general by any of the said Statutes of the said Kingdom, *and also all such Statutes in the Kingdom of England as declare the rights and liberties of the subjects and enact the better securing of the same,* and, also, so much of the said Statutes as relates to the above mentioned particulars of the allegiance of the people to their sovereign, the public oaths, and subscribing the tests required of them, *and the declaring and securing the rights and liberties of the subjects,* are hereby enacted and declared to extend to, and to be of full force in this province, as if particularly enumerated in this act.

Zenger's Case, New York, 1734 (Zenger, J. P., *Narrative of Case and Trial for Libel,* 1770; 1 Chandler, *American Criminal Trials* [1841], 151–207).

Cosby was appointed Governor of New York by the crown in 1732. He had a long voyage and it was some months before he arrived to take over his office. At that time officials were paid by fees provided by statutes for specific official acts. In the interval before Cosby reached New York one Van Dam collected the emoluments of the office and claimed he could keep them by virtue of a set-off for his work in performing the duties of the governor. Cosby claimed the emoluments belonged to him from the date of his appointment by virtue of his office. He saw that the local juries were not going to be favorable to him, so he conceived the idea of giving the Supreme Court of the Province equity jurisdiction so that it could try cases without a jury. He appointed and removed the judges. Indeed he removed the Chief Justice because the latter took a different view of the law from that held by the governor. If he could get the case before the judges without a jury he was assured of prevailing. When Van Dam tried to bring an action to establish his claim he found that he could not get process served because the governor controlled the administrative officers who alone could serve process. This was not the only high-handed thing the governor did. The provincial legislature between 1701 and 1728 had refused repeatedly to set up a court of equity. So Governor Cosby set one up of his own motion without any authority except his own, and the case against Van Dam was heard in this court although it was really a case for an action at law, not one for equity.

Zenger began to publish a newspaper in New York in 1733 and soon commented severely on the arbitrary acts of the governor, and especially on the Van Dam case and the way in which Governor Cosby had sought to evade trial by jury. In another article he wrote on freedome of the press and called attention to the operation of censorship under the governor. At the instance of the latter one of the justices of the Supreme Court charged the Grand Jury vigorously about seditious libel, but it refused to indict Zenger. However, the sheriff was under the control of the governor and the sheriff picked the Grand Jury. So at the next term the Chief Justice charged a picked grand jury vigorously about seditious libel and Zenger was indicted.

In those days law as well as facts was argued to juries. Andrew Hamilton, one of the great lawyers of that period, came on from Philadelphia and made a powerful argument based on Magna Carta and the common law as to the liberty of the subject. Zenger was acquitted.

Paxton's Case, Massachusetts, 1761 (Quincy, 51, 520–9).

[This was an application by an officer of the customs to the Superior Court for a writ of assistance, relying on an act of parliament. The significant feature is the argument of James Otis against the writ, relying on Bonham's Case, Day v. Savadge, and City of London v. Wood, quoted from Viner's Abridgment.

In his note to this case, Quincy, 512, 527, Gray says: "The same doctrine was repeatedly asserted by Otis and was a favorite in the colonies before the Revolution."

See also John Adams, *Works, 2,* 139, and the reference in Gray's note, supra, 527.]

In re Memorial of Boston, Massachusetts, 1765 (Quincy, 198–217).

[The Superior Courts, for want of stamp paper, required by the Stamp Act, ceased to do business from the time when the act was to have taken effect and continued all cases and matters pending before them to the next term. Thereupon the town of Boston presented a memorial to the governor in council saying: "We have always understood that the law is the great rule of right, the security of our lives and property, and the best birthright of Englishmen." The memorial asked to be heard by counsel and prayed the governor to give directions that the courts be opened.]

John Adams, for the Memorial: "The Stamp-Act, I take it, is utterly void, and of no binding Force upon us; for it is against our Rights as Men, and our Priviledges as Englishmen. An Act made in Defiance of the first Principles of Justice; an Act which rips up the Foundation of the British Constitution, and makes void Maxims of 1800 Years standing."

James Otis, also for the Memorial: ". . . Lawyers know that there are limits beyond which if parliaments go, their acts bind not." 4 Inst. 122 [i.e. Coke's Fourth Institute] . . . The "justices are commanded that they shall do even law and execution of right to all our subjects, rich and poor, without having regard to any person, without letting to do right for any letters or commandment which may come to them from us, or from any other, or by any other cause." 4 Inst. 70.

[The passage quoted by Otis from Coke's Fourth Institute is taken from a statute of Henry VIII, setting forth instructions to the justices.]

In re the Stamp Act, Virginia, 1766 (Wise, Note in 22 *Virginia Law Rev.* 103, 105–6).

Parliament passed the Stamp Act, and in May, 1765 Patrick Henry proceeded to assail it in the House of Burgesses. Sparing no effort to obtain a repeal of the measure, Benjamin Franklin aided by Pitt and other British Liberals even went before Parliament to plead the unwisdom of the new fiscal policy. Inasmuch as the Act was to go into effect on November 1, 1766, however, the Accomackians were not content with mere protests by Patrick Henry and Franklin.

Under the existing laws of Virginia the decisions of a County bench of Seven were entitled to full faith and credit by all the County courts of the Colony. Accordingly it was arranged by the sympathizers with Henry that the Clerk and officers of the court of Northampton County should present to the court of Northampton a petition requesting a formal ruling upon the constitutionality of the Act. When the petition was presented, the five justices were Littleton Eyre of "Eyre Hall," John Wilkins of "Drummondtown," John Bowdoin, John Stringer and Nathaniel Savage of "Savage's Neck." Adding Severn Eyre and John Harmonson to the bench as "special justices," on February 11, 1766 the Court by unanimous decision ruled "that *the said Act did not bind, effect, or concern the inhabitants of this Colony* inasmuch as they (the Court) conceived the said Act to be *unconstitutional.*" The opinion closed with the ruling that *"the said several officers may proceed in the execution of their respective offices without incurring any penalty by means thereof."*

This action constituted a case of unequivocal judicial review of [a statute contrary to] the English Constitution by a colonial court. It is all the more important because it did not merely decide the rights of the residents of Northampton County but of "His Majesty's subjects in the Colony of Virginia" as a whole.

The case and order are to be found in Northampton County Records, Order Book, 1766, P. 62.

Declaration of Rights of the Continental Congress, 1774.

Whereupon the deputies so appointed being now assembled in a full and free representation of these colonies, taking into their most serious consideration the best means of attaining the ends aforesaid, do in the first place, as Englishmen, their ancestors, in like cases have usually done, for asserting and vindicating their rights and liberties declare . . .

5. That the respective colonies are entitled to the common law of England and more especially to the great and inestimable privilege of being tried by their peers of the vicinage, according to the course of that law.

6. That they are entitled to the benefit of such of the English statutes as existed at the time of their colonization; and which they have, by experience, respectively found to be applicable to their several local and other circumstances.

Virginia, Declaration of Rights, January 12, 1776. (9 Hening, *Statutes at Large of Virginia*, 109–12. This the first American bill of rights).

1. That all men are by nature equally free and independent, and have certain inherent rights, of which, when they enter into a state of society, they cannot, by any compact, deprive or divest their posterity; namely, the enjoyment of life and liberty, with the means of acquiring and possessing property, and pursuing and obtaining happiness and safety.

2. That all power is vested in, and consequently derived from, the people; that magistrates are their trustees and servants, and at all times amenable to them.

3. That government is, or ought to be, instituted for the common benefit, protection, and security, of the people, nation, or community; of all the various modes and forms of government that is best, which is capable of producing the greatest degree of happiness and safety, and is most effectually secured against the danger of mal-administration; and that whenever any government shall be found inadequate or contrary to these purposes, a majority of the community hath an indubitable, unalienable, and indefeasible right, to reform, alter, or abolish it, in such manner as shall be judged most conducive to the public weal.

4. That no man, or set of men, are entitled to exclusive or separate emoluments or privileges from the community, but in consideration of publick services; which, not being descendible, neither ought the offices of magistrate, legislator, or judge to be hereditary.

5. That the legislative and executive powers of the state should be separate and distinct from the judiciary; and that the members of the two first may be restrained from oppression, by feeling and participating the burthens of the people, they should at fixed periods, be reduced to a private station, return into that body from which they were originally taken, and the vacancies be supplied by frequent, certain, and regular elections, in which all, or any part of the former members, to be again eligible, or ineligible, as the laws shall direct.

6. That elections of members to serve as representatives of the people, in assembly, ought to be free; and that all men, having sufficient evidence of permanent common interest with, and attachment to, the community, have the right of suffrage, and cannot be taxed or

deprived of their property for publick uses without their own consent, or that of their representatives so elected, nor bound by any law to which they have not, in like manner, assented, for the publick good.

7. That all power of suspending laws, or the execution of laws, by any authority, without consent of the representatives of the people, is injurious to their rights, and ought not to be exercised.

8. That in all capital or criminal prosecutions a man hath a right to demand the cause and nature of his accusation, to be confronted with the accusers and witnesses, to call for evidence in his favour, and to a speedy trial by an impartial jury of his vicinage, without whose unanimous consent he cannot be found guilty, nor can he be compelled to give evidence against himself; that no man be deprived of his liberty except by the law of the land, or the judgment of his peers.

9. That excessive bail ought not to be required, nor excessive fines imposed, nor cruel and unusual punishments inflicted.

10. That general warrants, whereby any officer or messenger may be commanded to search suspected places without evidence of a fact committed, or to seize any person or persons not named, or whose offence is not particularly described and supported by evidence, are grievous and oppressive, and ought not to be granted.

11. That in controversies respecting property, and in suits between man and man, the ancient trial by jury is preferable to any other, and ought to be held sacred.

12. That the freedom of the press is one of the great bulwarks of liberty, and can never be restrained but by despotick governments.

13. That a well regulated militia, composed of the body of the people, trained to arms, is the proper, natural, and safe defence of a free state; that standing armies, in time of peace, should be avoided, as dangerous to liberty; and that, in all cases, the military should be under strict subordination to, and governed by, the civil power.

14. That the people have a right to uniform government; and therefore, that no government separate from, or independent of, the government of Virginia, ought to be erected or established within the limits thereof.

15. That no free government, or the blessing of liberty, can be preserved to any people but by a firm adherence to justice, modera-

tion, temperance, frugality, and virtue, and by frequent recurrence to fundamental principles.

16. That religion, or the duty which we owe to our CREATOR, and the manner of discharging it, can be directed only by reason and conviction, not by force or violence, and therefore all men are equally entitled to the free exercise of religion, according to the dictates of conscience; and that it is the mutual duty of all to practise Christian forbearance, love, and charity, towards each other.

Maryland, Declaration of Rights, August 14, 1776 (sec. 3).

3. That the inhabitants of Maryland are entitled to the common law of England, and the trial by jury according to the course of that law, and to the benefit of such of the English statutes as existed at the time of their first emigration, and which by experience have been found applicable to their local and other circumstances, and of such others as have been since made in England or Great-Britain, and have been introduced, used and practised by the courts of law or equity.

Massachusetts, Declaration of Rights, 1780 (arts. X, XXX).

Art. X. Each individual of the society has a right to be protected by it in the enjoyment of his life, liberty, and property, according to standing laws. He is obliged, consequently, to contribute his share to the expense of this protection; to give his personal service, or an equivalent, when necessary; but no part of the property of any individual can, with justice, be taken from him, or applied to public uses, without his own consent, or that of the representative body of the people. In fine, the people of this commonwealth are not controllable by any other laws than those to which their constitutional representative body have given their consent. And whenever the public exigencies require that the property of any individual should be appropriated to public uses, he shall receive a reasonable compensation therefor.

Art. XXX. In the government of this commonwealth, the legislative department shall never exercise the executive and judicial powers, or either of them; the executive shall never exercise the legislative and judicial powers, or either of them; the judicial shall never exercise the legislative and executive powers, or either of them; to the end it may be a government of laws, and not of men.

Holmes v. Walton, Supreme Court of New Jersey, 1780 (Scott, Holmes v. Walton, The New Jersey Precedent, 4 *Am. Hist. Rev.* no. 3 (1899). See also Kirkpatrick, C. J., in State v. Parkhurst (1804), 4 Halst. (N.J.) 427, 444).

Section 22 of the Constitution of New Jersey (1776) provided that the "right of trial by jury shall remain confirmed as a part of the law of this colony without repeal forever." A statute of 1778 allowed a jury of six men in cases of seizure of goods brought from within the lines of the enemy or any place in the possession of the British. Under this act Walton, a major of militia, seized goods in the possession of Holmes whom he charged with having brought them within the lines of the enemy. On trial to a jury of six before Anderson, a justice of the peace, there was verdict and judgment for Walton. Holmes took the case to the Supreme Court on certiorari. The reasons urged for reversal of the judgment were:

> For that the said justice had not jurisdiction of the said cause or plaint but the same was *coram non judice*.[1]

> For that the jury who tried the said plaint before the said justice consisted of six men only contrary to law.

> For that the jury who tried the said plaint before the said justice consisted of six men only contrary to the constitution of New Jersey.

> For that the proceedings and trial in the said plaint in the court below, and the judgment thereon given were had and given contrary to the constitution, practices and laws of the land.

The case was decided September 7, 1780. The minute of the court reads thus: "John Holmes and Solomon Ketcham vs. Elisha Walton, sur certiorari to John Anderson, Esq. . . . This cause having been argued several terms past and the court having taken time to consider the same, and being now ready to deliver their opinion, gave the same seriatim for the plaintiffs in certiorari. And on motion of Boudinot for the plaintiffs, judgment is ordered for the plaintiffs, and that the judgment of the justice in the court below be reversed and the said plaintiffs be restored to all things, etc."

[1] Before one not a judge.

Commonwealth v. Caton, Court of Appeals of Virginia, 1782 (4 Call, 5).

The General Court having condemned Caton and others for treason, the House of Delegates granted them a pardon. The Attorney General moved in the General Court for execution of the judgment, whereupon the prisoners pleaded the pardon. The case was adjourned by the General Court to the Court of Appeals.

Wythe, J. . . . I have heard of an English Chancellor who said, and it was nobly said, that it was his duty to protect the rights of the subject against the encroachments of the Crown, and that he would do it, at every hazard. But if it was his duty to protect a solitary individual against the rapacity of the sovereign, surely, it is equally mine, to protect one branch of the legislature, and, consequently, the whole community, against the usurpations of the other; and, whenever the proper occasion occurs, I shall feel the duty, and fearlessly perform it. Whenever traitors shall be fairly convicted, by the verdict of their peers, before the competent tribunal, if one branch of the legislature, without the concurrence of the other, shall attempt to rescue the offenders from the sentence of the law, I shall not hesitate, sitting in this place, to say to the General Court, *Fiat justitia, ruat coelum;* [3] and, to the usurping branch of the legislature, you attempt worse than a vain thing; for although you cannot succeed, you set an example which may convulse society to its centre. Nay more, if the whole legislature, an event to be deprecated, should attempt to overleap the bounds prescribed to them by the people, I, in administering the public justice of the country, will meet the united powers at my seat in this tribunal; and, pointing to the Constitution, will say to them, here is the limit of your authority, and hither shall you go, but no further.

Waiving, however, longer discussion upon those subjects, and proceeding to the question immediately before us, the case presented is, that three men, convicted of treason against the State, and condemned by the General Court, have pleaded a pardon, by the House of Delegates, upon which that House insists, although the Senate refuses to concur; and the opinion of the court is asked, whether the General Court should award execution of the judgment, contrary to the allegation of the prisoners, that the House of Delegates alone

3. "Let justice be done though heaven fall."

have the power to pardon them, under that article of the Constitution which says, "But he (the Governor) shall, with the advice of the Council of State, have the power of granting reprieves or pardons, except where the prosecution shall have been carried on by the House of Delegates, or the law shall otherwise particularly direct; in which *cases*, no reprieve or pardon shall be granted, but by resolve of the House of Delegates."

Two questions are made:

1. Whether this court has jurisdiction in the case?

2. Whether the pardon is valid?

The first appears, to me, to admit of no doubt; for the Act constituting this court is express, that the court shall have jurisdiction "In such cases as shall be removed before them, by adjournment from the other courts before mentioned, when questions, in their opinion new and difficult, occur." Chan. Rev. 102; which emphatically embraces the case under consideration.

The sole inquiry therefore is, whether the pardon is valid?

If we consider the genius of our institutions, it is clear that the pretensions of the House of Delegates cannot be sustained. For, throughout the whole structure of government, concurrence of the several branches of each department is required to give effect to its operations. Thus the Governor, with the advice of the Council of State, may grant pardons, commission officers, and embody the militia; but he can do neither without the assent of the council: the two branches of the legislature may pass laws, but a bill passed by one of them has no force: and the two houses of assembly may elect a judge; but an appointment, by one of them only, would be useless. This general requisition of union seems of itself to indicate that nothing was intended to be done, in any department, without it; and, accordingly, the fourth section of the Constitution declares, that "The legislature shall be formed of two distinct branches, who, *together*, shall be a complete legislature;" and the eighth, "that all laws shall originate in the House of Delegates, to be approved or rejected by the Senate." Thus requiring, in conformity to the regulations throughout the whole fabric of government, an union of the two branches, to constitute a legislature; and an union of sentiment in the united body, to give effect to their acts. And it is not to be believed, that, when this union was so steadfastly demanded, even in the smallest cases, it was meant to be dispensed with, in one of the first magnitude, and which might involve the vital interests of the community. . .

Chancellor Blair and the rest of the judges were of opinion, that the court had power to declare any resolution or Act of the Legislature, or of either branch of it, to be unconstitutional and void; and that the resolution of the House of Delegates, in this case, was inoperative, as the Senate had not concurred in it. That this would be the consequence clearly if the words, "or the law shall otherwise particularly direct," were read in a parenthesis; for then the power of pardoning by the House of Delegates would be expressly confined to cases of impeachment by that House; and, if read without the parenthesis, then the only difference would be, that the assent of the two Houses would be necessary; for it would be absurd to suppose that it was intended by the Constitution that the Act of the whole Legislature should be repealed by the resolution of one branch of it, against the consent of the other.

The certificate of the General Court was as follows:—

"The court proceeded, pursuant to an order of the court of Thursday last, to render their judgment on the adjourned question, from the General Court, in the case of John Caton, Joshua Hopkins, and James Lamb; whereupon it is ordered to be certified, to the said General Court, as the opinion of this court, that the pardon, by resolution of the House of Delegates, severally pleaded and produced in the said court, by the said John Caton, Joshua Hopkins, and James Lamb, as by the record of their case appears, is invalid."

Symesbury Case, Superior Court of Connecticut, 1785 (Kirby, 444, 446).

[Action by the proprietors of Symesbury to recover land in the town of New Hartford described as in the original grant to Symesbury (1670). In 1686 there was a grant of lands west of Symesbury to the proprietors of Hartford and Windsor, under whom defendant claimed. In 1727 the General Assembly appointed Kimberly and others to survey the land later granted and the survey was afterwards "established" by the legislature. The case came up on demurrer.]

By the court: "The act of the General Assembly, confirming Kimberly's line, operated to restrict and limit the western extent of the jurisdiction of the town of Symsbury, but could not legally operate to curtail the land before granted to the proprietors of the town of Symsbury, without their consent; and the grant to Symsbury being prior to the grant made to the towns of Hartford and Windsor, under which the defendant claims, we are of opinion the title of the lands demanded is in the plaintiffs."

In a prior case involving the same question in the Supreme Court of Errors of Connecticut the presiding judge said: "I think it ought to be admitted in the case before us that the proprietors of Symesbury could not have their grant taken from them or curtailed, even by the General Assembly without their consent." [Idem, 45]

Trevett v. Weeden, Superior Court of Rhode Island, 1786 *

[A statute making paper money issued by the state legal tender provided a penalty for refusing to accept the bills as payment for goods offered for sale to be enforced summarily by a special court of at least three judges, without a jury "according to the laws of the land," with no continuance, "protection, privilege, or injunction," and no appeal.

The charter of Rhode Island, which then stood as its constitution, required statutes not to be "repugnant" to the laws of England.

Information by Trevett against Weeden for refusing to accept paper bills of the state in payment for meat sold. The judges unanimously held that the information was not cognizable before them.

Varnum, counsel for defendant, cited Bacon's *Abridgment* for the proposition that "if a statute . . . be repugnant, or impossible to be performed, the Common law shall control it, and adjudge it to be void." He maintained that the act of the general assembly is repugnant when it authorizes the judges to "proceed to trial without any jury, according to the laws of the land." The laws of the land constitute the jurors the triers of facts, and the judges the triers of law only. It was impossible that judges should try a man, without a jury, and at the same time try a man "according to the laws of the land,"

* (Varnum, James M. Case, Trevett against Weeden, for refusing paper bills in payment at par with specie, before the Superior Court, in the County of Newport, 1786; also the Case of the Judges of said court, before the General Assembly, 1786, for dismissing said complaint. Wherein the rights of the people to Trial by Jury are stated and the powers of government examined [1787]; 2 Chandler, *American Criminal Trials* [1844], 269–350).

which certainly secured to every freeman a trial "by the lawful judgment of his peers." Contraries could not exist and be executed at the same time. "This act therefore is impossible to be executed."

The following constitutes the whole of the brief extant report of what was said by them]:

The court adjourned to next morning, upon opening of which, Judge Howell, in a firm, sensible, and judicious speech, assigned the reasons which induced him to be of the opinion that the information was not cognizable by the court—declared himself independent as a judge—the penal law to be repugnant and unconstitutional—and therefore gave it as his opinion that the court could not take cognizance of the information! Judge Devol was of the same opinion. Judge Tillinghast took notice of the striking repugnancy of the expressions of the act—Without trial by jury, according to the laws of the land—and on that ground gave his judgment the same way. Judge Hazard voted against taking cognizance. The Chief Justice declared the judgment of the court without giving his own opinion.

Den d. Bayard v. Singleton, Court of Conference of North Carolina, 1787 (1 Martin N.C. 42).

Ejectment. This action was brought for the recovery of a valuable house and lot, with a wharf and other appurtenances, situate in the town of Newbern.

The defendant pleaded *Not guilty,* under the common rule.

He held under a title derived from the State, by a deed, from a Superintendent Commissioner of confiscated estates.

At May Term, 1786, Nash, for the defendant, moved that the suit be dismissed, according to an Act of the last session, entitled an Act to secure and quiet in their possession all such persons, their heirs and assigns, who have purchased or may hereafter purchase lands and tenements, goods and chattels, which have been sold or may hereafter be sold by commissioners of forefeited estates, legally appointed for that purpose, 1785, 7, 553.

The Act requires the courts, in all cases where the defendant makes affidavit that he holds the disputed property under a sale from a commissioner of forfeited estates, to dismiss the suit on motion.

The defendant had filed an affidavit, setting forth that the property in dispute had been confiscated and sold by the commissioner of the district.

This brought on long arguments from the counsel on each side, on constitutional points. . . .

At May Term, 1787, Nash's motion was resumed, and produced a very lenghty debate from the Bar.

Whereupon the court recommended to the parties to consent to a fair decision of the property in question, by a jury according to the common law of the land, and pointed out to the defendant the uncertainty that would always attend his title, if this cause should be dismissed without a trial; as upon a repeal of the present Act (which would probably happen sooner or later), suit might be again commenced against him for the same property, at the time when evidences, which at present were easy to be had, might be wanting. But this recommendation was without effect. . . .

The court, then, after every reasonable endeavor had been used in vain for avoiding a diagreeable difference between the legislature and the judicial powers of the State, at length with much apparent reluctance, but with great deliberation and firmness, gave their opinion separately, but unanimously, for overruling the aforementioned motion for the dismission of the said suits.

In the course of which the judges observed, that the obligation of their oaths, and the duty of their office required them, in that situation, to give their opinion on that important and momentous subject; and that notwithstanding the great reluctance they might feel against involving themselves in a dispute with the legislature of the State, yet no object of concern or respect could come in competition or authorize them to dispense with the duty they owed the public, in consequence of the trust they were invested with under the solemnity of their oaths.

That they therefore were bound to declare that they considered, that whatever disabilities the persons under whom the plaintiffs were said to derive their titles, might justly have incurred, against their maintaining or prosecuting any suits in the courts of this State; yet that such disabilities in their nature were merely personal, and not by any means capable of being transferred to the present plaintiffs, either by descent or purchase; and that these plaintiffs, being citizens of one of the United States, are citizens of this State, by the confederation of all the States; which is to be taken as a part of the law of the land, unrepealable by any Act of the General Assembly.

That by the Constitution every citizen had undoubtedly a right to a decision of his property by a trial by jury. For that if the legislature could take away this right, and require him to stand condemned in his property without a trial, it might with as much authority require his life to be taken away without a trial by jury, and that he should stand condemned to die, without the formality of any trial at all; that if the members of the General Assembly could do this, they might with equal authority, not only render themselves the legislators of the State for life, without any further election of the people, from thence transmit the dignity and authority of legislation down to their heirs male forever.

But that it was clear, that no Act they could pass, could by any means repeal or alter the Constitution, because, if they could do this, they would at the same instant of time destroy their own existence as a legislature, and dissolve the government thereby established. Consequently the Constitution (which the judicial power was bound to take notice of as much as of any other law whatever), standing in full force as the fundamental law of the land, notwithstanding the Act on which the present motion was grounded, the same act must of course, in that instance, stand as abrogated and without any effect.

Nash's motion was overruled.

Bowman v. Middleton, Superior Court of South Carolina, 1792 (1 Bay, 252).

The only point of law of any importance which occurred in the course of the trial was a title, set up under an act of assembly passed so long since as in the year 1712. From the ancient grants and papers produced, it appeared, that in August, 1677, one Roger Nicholls obtained a grant for 510 acres of land on Ashley river. That in 1701, John Cattell, the father of William Cattel, (under whom the plaintiffs claimed,) obtained a grant for 240 acres, on Ashley river, adjoining Nicholls'; but, from the examination of the plots, it appeared that the grant to John Cattel ran into Nicholls' land so far as to include 146 acres of his tract. John Cattel soon after died intestate. In 1712 an act was passed confirming the right and title of John, William, Benjamin, and Peter, sons of John Cattel, deceased, and John minor grandson of old John Cattel, of, in, and to, sundry tracts of land, in the said act particularly mentioned; and, among others, this tract of 240 acres on Ashley river, which had been run out by old John Cattel, in 1701, was confirmed by William Cattel, the second son, his heirs and assigns forever. Under this act, therefore, the plaintiffs claimed 240 acres of the land in dispute, being part and parcel of the 490 acres sold.

For the defendant, an objection was taken by his counsel, that no title could be transferred by this act. That it was against common right and reason as well as against *magna charta;* therefore, *ipso facto,* void. In the first place, it went to deprive the heir at law of Nicholls of 146 acres of land, without being called upon to answer or defend his title; and that too without the intervention of a trial by his peers. In the next place, it went to deprive the eldest son of old John Cattel of his inheritance, (his father dying intestate,) by settling the estate in William, the second son. So that, in fact, it wrought a two-fold injury, by depriving the heir at law of Nicholls and the heir at law of Cattel of their freeholds, without a trial by jury. They admitted that there might be great and urgent occasions wherein it might be justifiable for the state to take private property from individuals, (upon a full indemnification,) for the purposes of fortifications or public works, &c. but in no case could the legislature of the country interfere with private property, by taking it from one man and giving it to another, to the prejudice of either party, or that of third persons, who might be interested in the event. That the courts of justice were always open to give redress, and determine on the right; and that these courts were the proper tribunals to apply to for redress in such cases.

This point, without further argument, was submitted to

The Court, (present, Grimke and Bay, Justices,) who, after a full consideration on the subject, were clearly of opinion, that the plaintiffs could claim no title under the act in question, as it was against common right, as well as against *magna charta,* to take away the freehold of one man and vest it in another, and that, too, to the prejudice of third persons, without any compensation, or even a trial by the jury of the country, to determine the right in question. That the act was, therefore, *ipso facto,* void. That no length of time could give it validity, being originally founded on erroneous principles. That the parties, however, might, if they chose, rely upon a possessory right, if they could establish it.

Constitution of the United States, 1787 (excerpts).

Art. I. § 9. (2). The Privilege of the Writ of Habeas Corpus shall not be suspended, unless when in Cases of Rebellion or Invasion the public Safety may require it.

(3.) No Bill of Attainder or ex post facto Law shall be passed.

Art. I, § 10. (1.) No State shall enter into any Treaty, Alliance, or Confederation; grant Letters of Marque and Reprisal; coin Money; emit Bills of Credit; make any Thing but gold and silver Coin a Tender in Payment of Debts; pass any Bill of Attainder, ex post facto Law, or Law impairing the Obligation of Contracts, or grant any Title of Nobility.

Art. VI. (2.) This Constitution, and the Laws of the United States which shall be made in Pursuance thereof; and all Treaties made, or which shall be made, under the Authority of the United States, shall be the supreme Law of the Land; and the Judges in every State shall be bound thereby, any Thing in the Constitution or Laws of any State to the Contrary notwithstanding.

Bill of Rights (first nine amendments).

Art. I. Congress shall make no law respecting an establishment of religion, or prohibiting the free exercise thereof; or abridging the freedom of speech, or of the press; or the right of the people peaceably to assemble, and to petition the Government for a redress of grievances.

Art. II. A well regulated Militia, being necessary to the security of a free State, the right of the people to keep and bear Arms, shall not be infringed.

Art. III. No Soldier shall, in time of peace be quartered in any house, without the consent of the Owner, nor in time of war, but in a manner to be prescribed by law.

Art. IV. The right of the people to be secure in their persons, houses, papers, and effects, against unreasonable searches and seizures, shall not be violated, and no Warrants shall issue, but upon probable cause, supported by Oath or affirmation, and particularly describing the place to be searched, and the persons or things to be seized.

Art. V. No person shall be held to answer for a capital, or otherwise infamous crime, unless on a presentment or indictment of a Grand Jury, except in cases arising in the land or naval forces, or in the Militia, when in actual service in time of War or public danger; nor shall any person be subject for the same offence to be twice put in jeopardy of life or limb; nor shall be compelled in any criminal case to be a witness against himself, nor be deprived of life, liberty, or property, without due process of law; nor shall private property be taken for public use, without just compensation.

Art. VI. In all criminal prosecutions the accused shall enjoy the right to a speedy and public trial, by an impartial jury of the State and district wherein the crime shall have been previously ascertained by law, and to be informed of the nature and cause of the accusation; to be confronted with the witnesses against him; to have compulsory process for obtaining witnesses in his favor, and to have the Assistance of Counsel for his defence.

Art. VII. In suits at common law, where the value in controversy shall exceed twenty dollars, the right of trial by jury shall be preserved, and no fact tried by a jury shall be otherwise re-examined in any Court of the United States, than according to the rules of the common law.

Art. VIII. Excessive bail shall not be required, nor excessive fines imposed, nor cruel and unusual punishments inflicted.

Art. IX. The enumeration in the Constitution, of certain rights, shall not be construed to deny or disparage others retained by the people.

Index

Absolute monarchy, 13

Absolutism, cult of, 109

Accused persons: counsel for, 89; right to witnesses, 86; rights of, 154–8, 188; safeguards of, 85

Acton, Lord, 4

Adams, John, 61, 64, 73, 75, 79, 80, 185

Administrative agencies, 86

Administrative regime, constitutional, 111

Admiralty jurisdiction, 71

Almon, 68

Analytical theory, purpose of, 94, 95

Anglo-Saxon laws, 52

Aristotle, 6, 29, 95, 137

Articles of the Barons, 15, 76, 108

Articles of Confederation, 65

Assembly, right of, 166

Assize of Clarendon, 113

Athon, *Constitutiones*, 132

Atkyns, Sir Robert, 40

Australia, 78; Constitution of, 110

Authority, legal limits of, 103

Bacon, 38, 43–4

Bacon's Abridgment, 99, 194

Bail, excessive, 87, 88

Balance, idea of, 2, 3

Balance between general security and individual life, 87

Bayard v. Singleton, 100, 195–6

Bedloe, 39

Benevolences, 166, 168

Bertie, Sir Vere, 39

Bible, interpretation of, 30

Bill of attainder, 107, 199

Bill of Pains and Penalties, 83, 107

Bill of Rights, 47; American, 82–9; as bill of liberties, 92; as exhortation, 101; idea of, 83; model of, 83; nature of, 92

Bill of Rights (English), 54, 62, 72, 75, 76, 84, 85, 87, 88, 90, 179–82; (Federal), 64, 84, 86, 87, 88, 89, 90, 107, 108, 199–200

Blackstone, 54, 57, 61, 70, 74

Blair, John, 99

Board of Trade and Plantations, 56, 76, 85

Bonham's Case, 51, 73, 79, 99, 171–4

Boston, 80; memorial of, 185

Bowman v. Middleton, 197–8

Bracton, 9, 27, 46, 129, 166

Bramston, Sir Francis, 39

Brandeis, Mr. Justice, 94

Campbell v. Hall, 63

Canada, Constitution of, 110

Canon law, 131, 132

Canterbury, Archbishop of, 45

Cavendish, Case of, 34–5, 142–5

Censorship, 69

Centralization of power, 93, 103

Charles I, 39, 46, 47, 84

Charles II, 38, 39

Charles V, 29

Charter, idea of, 82

Charter of Liberties, 15, 16, 17, 112–13

Christendom, medieval theory of, 10, 11

Citizens, privileges and immunities of, 84

City of London v. Wood, 53, 73, 79, 178

City-state, 5

Civil law, 7, 28, 110
Civil liberties, British idea of, v
Civilization, 3
Coke, Sir Edward, 2, 32, 33, 37, 38, 43–50, 72, 79, 96, 99, 103; Commentary on Magna Carta, 47, 48, 107, 108, 148–62; Fourth Institute, 185; idea of liberty, 66; Second Institute, 47, 48, 50, 57, 60, 63, 65, 66, 72, 73, 78
Collector of taxes, authority of, 23, 131
Colonial charters, provisions of, 182–3
Colonial courts, appeals from, 77
Colonial legislation: validity of, 81; veto of, 75
Colonies: American, 55; grievances of, 71–4; proprietary, 92; relation to home government, 55, 56
Common law, 7
Common law compared with civil law, 136–7
Common Pleas, Court of, 25, 26, 45
Commonwealth, 82; English, 62
Commonwealth v. Caton, 98, 191–3
Confirmation of charters, 23, 129, 130
Confrontation with witnesses, 85
Connecticut, 82, 86
Constantine, 10
Constitution, 47, 65; as a legal document, 102; as supreme law of the land, 96, 110; both legal and political, 102; enforceable as law, 110; grants of power in, 105; guarantees of, 105; legal precepts of, 104; limitations in, 105; principles in, 105–6; prohibitions in, 105
Constitutional government, vitality of, 110, 111
Constitutional guarantees, periods in development of, 2
Constitutional ideas, types of, 102
Constitutional law, 49, 77, 103; task of, 104

Constitutional provisions, types of, 103, 104
Constitutions, Continental and Latin American, 105
Continental Congress, 64, 82; Declaration of Rights by, 2
Cosby, Governor, 69, 70
Court of Requests, 28
Courts: contests with crown, 102; of common law, 15; struggle with Parliament, 25, 26
Crewe, Sir Randolph, 39
Criminal investigation: abuses in, 89; restrictions on, 87
Cromwell, 40
Crown, criticism of, 67
Cruel and unusual punishments, 87, 181, 200
Custom, medieval faith in, 7

D'Aguesseau, 10
Darcy v. Allen, 36, 37, 145–8
Day v. Savadge, 51, 52, 73, 74, 79, 175–6
Declaration of Independence, 47, 59, 60, 75, 81, 82, 85
Declaration of Indulgence, 68
Declaration of Rights, 64, 75, 77; of Continental Congress, 186; of Maryland, 189; of Massachusetts, 189; of Virginia, 187–9
Declaration of the Rights of Man (French), 102
Decretals of Gregory IX, 132
Delaware, 82
Democracy, constitutional, 111
Devonshire, Earl of, 84
Digest of Justinian, 9
Dispensing power, 40, 52, 88, 179, 181
Dissenters, 58
District, arbitrary, 89
Domesday Book, 11
Dooley, Martin, 56
Double jeopardy, 83, 200
Due process of law, 48, 50, 153, 200

Dulany, Daniel, Jr., 59
Dulany, Daniel, Sr., 59, 64

Edward I, 22, 23, 25, 28, 31, 75
Edward II, 31, 48
Edward III, 33
Eire, 78; Constitution of, 110
Eldon, Lord, 44
Elizabeth, Queen, 30, 32, 34, 36, 45
Emigration, right of, 84
Empson, 145
Empson & Dudley, 32, 33, 72, 154
English statutes, benefit of, 186, 189
Englishmen, guaranteed rights of, 48
Equity jurisdiction, 52
Excessive bail, 180, 181, 188, 200
Excessive fines, 180, 181, 200
Executive, as judge of its own powers, 9
Ex post facto laws, 88
Experience as basis of constitutional limitations, 102

False imprisonment, 157-9
Fifth Amendment, 2, 105
Fines, excessive, 84
First Amendment, 65
Fitzhugh, William, 59
Forced loans, 166
Forfeitures, grants of, 182
Fortescue, 25, 30, 108; De laudibus legum Angliae, 136-42
Fourteenth Amendment, 2, 65, 66, 106
Francis I, 29
Freedom: as an end, 3; of assembly, 199; of elections, 181, 187; of petition, 199; of the press, 85; of religion, 65, 189, 199; of speech, 65, 66, 70, 71, 181, 199; of speech, in colonies, 69
Fundamental law, 8, 61, 78, 91, 101, 110, 153

General security, 4
General warrants, 188
Georgia, 81, 84, 89, 92

Germanic polity, 6, 8
Government: arbitrary acts of, 103; authority of, 41; centralization of powers of, 71; end of, 109; feudal idea of, 11; Germanic idea of, 12; limitations on, 55, 56; political idea of, 11; Roman idea of, 12
Governor and Council in colonies, 93
Governor's Council, powers of, 76, 77
Grand Jury, 67, 70, 83, 200
Gratian, Decretum of, 131, 132
Gray, Mr. Justice, 79
Gray's Inn, 59
Greek city-state, 5
Greek philosophers, 5
Gridley, Jeremy, 73, 79
Grotius, 74
Guarantees of liberty: as exhortations, v, 8; as law of the land, v; as precepts of law, 8; as pronouncement of political ethics, v; medieval, 9

Habeas Corpus, 86, 88, 159, 199
Habeas Corpus Act, 63
Halifax, Lord, 60
Hamilton, Andrew, 59, 64, 71
Hampden, 49-50
Hatton, Sir Christopher, 35
Hellenistic era, 5
Henry I, 14, 15, 16
Henry II, 17, 21, 22, 46; achievements of, 18
Henry III, 22, 29
Henry V, 26
Henry VI, 25
Henry VII, 30, 32, 33
Henry VIII, 28, 30, 31, 33
Herbert, Sir Edward, 40, 41
High Commission, 45
High Commission, Court of, 43, 181
Hobart, Chief Justice, 53, 74
Holmes v. Walton, 97, 190
Holt, Lord, 52, 53, 176
Hutchinson, Governor, 79

Individual: primacy of, 103; security of, 139–42
Information, *ex officio*, 67
Inner Temple, 60
Inns of Court, 59, 60, 61, 73
Instincts, 3
Institutes of Justinian, 9
Instrument of Government, 62, 82, 96
Intermountain Rate Cases, 95
Interpretation: judicial, 104; confusion with application, 104; difficulties of, 104; not wholly logical, 104
Interstate Commerce Commission, 95

Jackson, Mr. Justice, v
James I, 37, 45, 46, 47; Conference with Judges, 45–6, 163–6
James II, 38, 40, 41, 44, 52, 68, 84, 87, 88
Jhering, 14
John, 18, 20, 21
Jones, Sir Thomas, 37, 40, 41
Jonson, Ben, 44
Judge: as delegate of King, 8, 163; as party, 51–5, 172–4, 176, 178–9
Judges: advance opinions of, 38; colonial, 76; impartial, guaranty of, 84; independence of, 84; removal of, 37, 39; salaries of, 84
Judiciary, independence of, 77, 93
Junius, 68
Jurisdiction, distinguished from ownership, 12
Jury, 68; trial by, 71, 85, 101, 151–3, 186, 188, 190, 200
Justice: administration of, 5; delay of, 160; denial of, 88, 161–2; magisterial, 58
Justiciar, 13
Justinian, 6, 10, 29

Kant, 1, 3
King: as fountain of justice, 13; as judge, 8, 163–5; as patriarchal head, 4; as source of jurisdiction, 12; authority of in England, 136–40; authority of in France, 136–40; dispensing power of, 40; divine right of, 41; interference with courts of justice, 24
King v. Earl of Banbury, 52, 53, 176–8
King's Bench, Court of, 15, 23
King's Council, 28
King's Courts, 15

Lambert MSS, 79
Land bill, 113–15
Law: as academic tradition, 11; as custom, 11; as product of courts, 10, 11; as product of universities, 10, 11; as quest of justice and truth, 9; as will of Emperor, 9; medieval faith in, vi; medieval idea of, 9; positive, 74; supremacy of, 20
Law book, first American, 62–3
Law of the land, 47, 55, 61, 78, 101, 148–9, 153–8
Laws: ex post facto, 88, 199; retrospective, 88; suspension of, 88, 181, 188
Lawyers: American, 57, 61, 63–4; Cavalier, 57; colonial, 56; English trained, 59–60, 61, 73; in constitutional convention, 110; lay idea of, 58; Maryland, 60; need for, 58
Legal ideas, medieval, 103
Legal order, Roman theory of, 7
Legal question, relation to political, 102
Legal theory, American, 57
Legislation: against common right and reason, 78; by proclamation, 29; colonial, 58; impertinent to be observed, 78; unconstitutional, 78; veto by Privy Council, 92
Legislative lynchings, 107
Legislature, arbitrary action of in formative era, 101
Leicester, Earl of, 35

Lettres de cachet, 24
Libel, 67, 70, 71
Liberty: as birthright of Americans, 2; common-law tradition of, 28; Kantian idea of, 1; meaning of, 1, 48, 109, 110, 150; unlawful restraint of, 37
Life, liberty, and property, security of, 86
Lindwood *provinciale*, 132
London, custom of, 162
Long Parliament, 39, 79
Lord and man, relation of, 12
Lord Cromwell's Case, 50, 169–71
Lynching, 87

McCardie, Mr. Justice, 84
Magna Carta, 15, 29, 33, 34, 35, 41, 47, 49, 54, 56, 63, 73, 75, 79, 88, 90, 99, 101, 102, 103, 108, 117–28, 167–8; as legal document, 19; as redress of grievances, 21; custom of London, 119, 120; established system of constitutional government, 22; ground plan of, 18; guarantees in, 118; judgment by one's peers, 126, 151; justice not to be sold, denied, or delayed, 123; nature of, 20; no excessive fines, 125; reasonable incidents of tenure, 118, 119, 120; reissue of, 128; roots of, 19, 20, 32; security of the person, 123, 125, 166, 167, 168; security of property, 124, 125, 126, 167; security of trade and commerce, 123
Majority, absolute rule of, 109
Mansfield, Lord, 63
Marshall, John, 94, 105
Martial law, 168–9
Mary, Queen, 30, 33
Maryland, 59, 76, 81, 82, 84, 85, 86, 87, 88, 89
Mason, George, 59
Massachusetts, 60, 72, 73, 81, 84, 85, 86, 87, 89, 90
Middle Temple, 59

Military power, subordination to civil power, 89, 188
Military tribunals, 4
Militia, 91, 188, 199
Miller, Mr. Justice, 109
Milton, 44
Mirror of Justices, 12
Monarchy, constitutional, 111
Monopolies, 46, 48, 84, 162
Monopoly, royal grant of, 36, 37
Montagu, Sir William, 40
Montesquieu, 95, 96
Mosaic law, 58

Napoleon III, 9
Natural law, 9, 10
Natural rights, 74, 79; theory of, 73, 74
Navigation Acts, 72
Nerford's Case, 23, 131
New England, 58, 72
New Hampshire, 72, 82, 84, 85, 86, 87, 88, 89
New Jersey, 82
New York, 60
Newgate, 87
Norman Conquest, 6
North Carolina, 60, 82, 84, 85, 86, 87, 88, 89, 90
Northampton County, Va., 80
Novanglus, 75

Obligation of contract, impairment of, 199
Offices, property in, 34, 35
Officials, dignity of, 66; legal responsibility of, 111
Oklahoma, 2
Otis, James, 60, 64, 72, 73, 78, 79, 80, 185

Parliament: acts of "impertinent to be observed," 96; authority of, 25–6, 54; criticism of, 67; High Court of, 15; sole power of to raise money, 33; void acts of, 173–4, 176, 177, 179
Paxton's Case, 78, 79, 184–5

Peacham, 38
Pemberton, Sir Francis, 40
Penalties, proportional, 84
Pendleton, Edward, 60
Pennsylvania, 59, 81, 82, 83, 86, 87, 89, 90; denied system of courts, 92
Person, security of, 148–50, 160, 165, 199
Petition of Right, 47, 63, 75, 76, 84, 166, 181; right of, 72
Philadelphia, 59
Philip and Mary, 33
Philosophers, medieval, 12
Physicians, Royal College of, 51
Plantagenets, 30
Power: concentration of, 76; tendency of to corrupt, 4
Powers: centralization of, 85, 96; separation of, 77, 85, 91–6, 187, 189
Powys, argument of, 73
Preamble, 37, 147
Prerogatives, 30, 33, 49, 52, 55, 108, 180, 181
Prior of Castleacre's Case, 133–6
Privy Council, 56, 58, 62, 67, 76, 77, 78, 81, 85, 92; interference in litigation, 93; judicial committee of, 110
Prohibition, Case of, 163
Property: security of, 139–45, 148–9; taking of for public use, 83, 108, 187–8, 200
Prosecution, political, 85
Protection, royal, 161
Protestant, 90
Public law, 102
Punishments, cruel and unusual, 87, 181, 200
Puritan Revolution, 90, 102

Quincy's Reports, 79
Quod principi placuit legis habet vigorem, 136–7

Rainsford, Sir Richard, 39
Randolph, Sir John, 59

Reformation, 20, 26, 27, 66, 73
Religion, freedom of, 189
Renaissance, 27, 74
Restoration, 67
Revolution: of 1688, 54; American, 54; English, 67, 90; right of, 90
Rhode Island, 81, 82
Richard II, 31, 50
Right of assembly, 72
Right to bear arms, 90, 91, 180, 181, 199
Rights: as heritage of Americans, 103; common-law, 64, 74–5, 186; natural, 64; philosophical basis of, 96; retained by the people, 200; secured by Magna Carta, 22
Roman law, 6, 7, 10; reception of, 27, 28
Rous v. Abbot, 132–3
Royal governors, 85, 87; instructions to, 72
Russell, Lord, 40
Rutledge, John, 60

Saint Asaph, Dean of, 68
Saint Augustine, 5
Scroggs, Sir William, 39, 67
Savannah, Town Court of, 92
Searches and seizures, 89; unreasonable, 199
Security of property, 189, 194, 198, 200
Self-incrimination, immunity from, 86
Separation of powers, 91–6, 187, 189; attacks upon, 95, 96; difficulties of, 94–6; experience behind, 93; historical view of, 95; reason for, 93–4
Seven Bishops, trial of, 68
Shakespeare, 29
Ship money, case of, 49
Social control, 3
Social order, postulates of, 3
Society: frontier, 58; kin-organized, 4; politically organized, 4, 5; relational organization of, 29, 58

Socrates, 6
Soldiers, quartering of, 84, 167, 199
South Africa, 78
South African Republic, 90, 110
South Carolina, 60, 64, 86, 89, 101
Stamp Act, 49, 60, 64, 67, 79, 80, 185–6; Case (Va.), 185–6
Standards, 106; application of, 106–7
Standing army, 180, 181
Star Chamber, 28, 66, 67
Stavisky scandal, 93
Story, Joseph, 91
Stuarts, 31, 68, 101, 109
Sub Deo et lege, 166
Supreme law of the land, 199
Symesbury Case, 99, 194–5

Taxation, 16; without authority of Parliament, 166, 167, 181; without representation, 71, 72
Tenth Amendment, 105
Tenure, incidents of, 17
Test Acts, 40
Thurland, Sir Edward, 39
Treason, 155
Trevett v. Weeden, 99, 194–5
Trial, in the vincinage, 89
Tucker, John Randolph, 107

Tudors, 30, 31, 108
Tyburn, 87

Uitlanders, 90
Unconstitutional legislation, judicial power over, 97–101, 191–8
Universality, ideal of, 11

Van Dam, 69, 70
Viner's Abridgment, 70
Virginia, 59, 81, 82, 85, 86, 87, 88, 89; County Court of, 80

Walter, Sir John, 39
Warrant, requirement of, 23, 131, 155–9
Warrants, general, 86, 188, 199
Wars of the Roses, 29
Westminster, concentration of power at, 92
Whippings, 87
Wilde, Sir William, 39
Wilkes, John, 68
William I, 11, 14, 16
William III, 40, 69
William Rufus, 14, 15
Wilson, James, 90
Witnesses, process for, 86
Wythe, George, 59, 99, 191

Zenger, John Peter, 59, 64, 69–71
Zenger's Case, 77, 85, 183–4

THE YALE PAPERBOUNDS

Y–1   LIBERAL EDUCATION AND THE DEMOCRATIC IDEAL by A. Whitney Griswold

Y–2   A TOUCH OF THE POET by Eugene O'Neill

Y–3   THE FOLKLORE OF CAPITALISM by Thurman Arnold

Y–4   THE LOWER DEPTHS AND OTHER PLAYS by Maxim Gorky

Y–5   THE HEAVENLY CITY OF THE EIGHTEENTH-CENTURY PHILOSOPHERS by Carl Becker

Y–6   LORCA by Roy Campbell

Y–7   THE AMERICAN MIND by Henry Steele Commager

Y–8   GOD AND PHILOSOPHY by Etienne Gilson

Y–9   SARTRE by Iris Murdoch

Y–10   AN INTRODUCTION TO THE PHILOSOPHY OF LAW by Roscoe Pound

Y–11   THE COURAGE TO BE by Paul Tillich

Y–12   PSYCHOANALYSIS AND RELIGION by Erich Fromm

Y–13   BONE THOUGHTS by George Starbuck

Y–14   PSYCHOLOGY AND RELIGION by C. G. Jung

Y–15   EDUCATION AT THE CROSSROADS by Jacques Maritain

Y–16   LEGENDS OF HAWAII by Padraic Colum

Y–17   AN INTRODUCTION TO LINGUISTIC SCIENCE by E. H. Sturtevant

Y–18   A COMMON FAITH by John Dewey

Y–19   ETHICS AND LANGUAGE by Charles L. Stevenson

Y–20   BECOMING by Gordon W. Allport

Y–21   THE NATURE OF THE JUDICIAL PROCESS by Benjamin N. Cardozo

Y–22   PASSIVE RESISTANCE IN SOUTH AFRICA by Leo Kuper

Y–23   THE MEANING OF EVOLUTION by George Gaylord Simpson

Y–24   PINCKNEY'S TREATY by Samuel Flagg Bemis

Y–25   TRAGIC THEMES IN WESTERN LITERATURE edited by Cleanth Brooks

Y–26   THREE STUDIES IN MODERN FRENCH LITERATURE by J. M. Cocking, Enid Starkie, and Martin Jarrett-Kerr

Y–27   WAY TO WISDOM by Karl Jaspers

Y–28   DAILY LIFE IN ANCIENT ROME by Jérôme Carcopino

Y–29   THE CHRISTIAN IDEA OF EDUCATION edited by Edmund Fuller

Y–30   FRIAR FELIX AT LARGE by H. F. M. Prescott

Y–31   THE COURT AND THE CASTLE by Rebecca West

Y–32   SCIENCE AND COMMON SENSE by James B. Conant

Y–33   THE MYTH OF THE STATE by Ernst Cassirer

Y–34 FRUSTRATION AND AGGRESSION *by John Dollard et al.*

Y–35 THE INTEGRATIVE ACTION OF THE NERVOUS SYSTEM *by Sir Charles Sherrington*

Y–36 TOWARD A MATURE FAITH *by Erwin R. Goodenough*

Y–37 NATHANIEL HAWTHORNE *by Randall Stewart*

Y–38 POEMS *by Alan Dugan*

Y–39 GOLD AND THE DOLLAR CRISIS *by Robert Triffin*

Y–40 THE STRATEGY OF ECONOMIC DEVELOPMENT *by Albert O. Hirschman*

Y–41 THE LONELY CROWD *by David Riesman*

Y–42 LIFE OF THE PAST *by George Gaylord Simpson*

Y–43 A HISTORY OF RUSSIA *by George Vernadsky*

Y–44 THE COLONIAL BACKGROUND OF THE AMERICAN REVOLUTION *by Charles M. Andrews*

Y–45 THE FAMILY OF GOD *by W. Lloyd Warner*

Y–46 THE MAKING OF THE MIDDLE AGES *by R. W. Southern*

Y–47 THE DYNAMICS OF CULTURE CHANGE *by Bronislaw Malinowski*

Y–48 ELEMENTARY PARTICLES *by Enrico Fermi*

Y–49 SWEDEN: THE MIDDLE WAY *by Marquis W. Childs*

Y–50 JONATHAN DICKINSON'S JOURNAL *edited by Evangeline Walker Andrews and Charles McLean Andrews*

Y–51 MODERN FRENCH THEATRE *by Jacques Guicharnaud*

Y–52 AN ESSAY ON MAN *by Ernst Cassirer*

Y–53 THE FRAMING OF THE CONSTITUTION OF THE UNITED STATES *by Max Farrand*

Y–54 JOURNEY TO AMERICA *by Alexis de Tocqueville*

Y–55 THE HIGHER LEARNING IN AMERICA *by Robert M. Hutchins*

Y–56 THE VISION OF TRAGEDY *by Richard B. Sewall*

Y–57 MY EYES HAVE A COLD NOSE *by Hector Chevigny*

Y–58 CHILD TRAINING AND PERSONALITY *by John W. M. Whiting and Irvin L. Child*

Y–59 RECEPTORS AND SENSORY PERCEPTION *by Ragnar Granit*

Y–60 VIEWS OF JEOPARDY *by Jack Gilbert*

Y–61 LONG DAY'S JOURNEY INTO NIGHT *by Eugene O'Neill*

Y–62 JAY'S TREATY *by Samuel Flagg Bemis*

Y–63 SHAKESPEARE: A BIOGRAPHICAL HANDBOOK *by Gerald Eades Bentley*

Y–64 THE POETRY OF MEDITATION *by Louis L. Martz*

Y–65 SOCIAL LEARNING AND IMITATION *by Neal E. Miller and John Dollard*

Y–66 LINCOLN AND HIS PARTY IN THE SECESSION CRISIS *by David M. Potter*

Y–67   SCIENCE SINCE BABYLON by Derek J. de Solla Price
Y–68   PLANNING FOR FREEDOM by Eugene V. Rostow
Y–69   BUREAUCRACY by Ludwig von Mises
Y–70   JOSIAH WILLARD GIBBS by Lynde Phelps Wheeler
Y–71   HOW TO BE FIT by Robert Kiphuth
Y–72   YANKEE CITY by W. Lloyd Warner
Y–73   WHO GOVERNS? by Robert A. Dahl
Y–74   THE SOVEREIGN PREROGATIVE by Eugene V. Rostow
Y–75   THE PSYCHOLOGY OF C. G. JUNG by Jolande Jacobi
Y–76   COMMUNICATION AND PERSUASION by Carl I. Hovland, Irving L. Janis, and Harold H. Kelley
Y–77   IDEOLOGICAL DIFFERENCES AND WORLD ORDER edited by F. S. C. Northrop
Y–78   THE ECONOMICS OF LABOR by E. H. Phelps Brown
Y–79   FOREIGN TRADE AND THE NATIONAL ECONOMY by Charles P. Kindleberger
Y–80   VOLPONE edited by Alvin B. Kernan
Y–81   TWO EARLY TUDOR LIVES edited by Richard S. Sylvester and Davis P. Harding
Y–82   DIMENSIONAL ANALYSIS by P. W. Bridgman
Y–83   ORIENTAL DESPOTISM by Karl A. Wittfogel
Y–84   THE COMPUTER AND THE BRAIN by John von Neumann
Y–85   MANHATTAN PASTURES by Sandra Hochman
Y–86   CONCEPTS OF CRITICISM by René Wellek
Y–87   THE HIDDEN GOD by Cleanth Brooks
Y–88   THE GROWTH OF THE LAW by Benjamin N. Cardozo
Y–89   THE DEVELOPMENT OF CONSTITUTIONAL GUARANTEES OF LIBERTY by Roscoe Pound
Y–90   POWER AND SOCIETY by Harold D. Lasswell and Abraham Kaplan
Y–91   JOYCE AND AQUINAS by William T. Noon, S.J.
Y–92   HENRY ADAMS: SCIENTIFIC HISTORIAN by William Jordy
Y–93   THE PROSE STYLE OF SAMUEL JOHNSON by William K. Wimsatt, Jr.
Y–94   BEYOND THE WELFARE STATE by Gunnar Myrdal
Y–95   THE POEMS OF EDWARD TAYLOR edited by Donald E. Stanford
Y–96   ORTEGA Y GASSET by José Ferrater Mora
Y–97   NAPOLEON: FOR AND AGAINST by Pieter Geyl
Y–98   THE MEANING OF GOD IN HUMAN EXPERIENCE by William Ernest Hocking
Y–99   THE VICTORIAN FRAME OF MIND by Walter E. Houghton
Y–100 POLITICS, PERSONALITY, AND NATION BUILDING by Lucian W. Pye